THE ESSENCE OF THE HINDU RELIGION

With an Introduction to the VEDAS and YOGA

Sudhir Anand

ASK Publications ● Los Angeles

The Cover
The figure ॐ is an alphabet letter in Sanskrit,
which would be written as Om in English. Om is the name
of God in the Hindu religion.

Published by:

ASK Publications
Post Office Box 29182
Los Angeles, CA 90029-0182
TEL/FAX: (323) 664-8078
E-mail: askpublications@yahoo.com

Copyright © 2000 Sudhir Anand
Second Printing 2001

All Rights Reserved

Publisher's Cataloging-in-Publication
(Provided by Quality Books, Inc.)
Anand, Sudhir.
    The essence of the Hindu religion : with an
    introduction to the Vedas and yoga / Sudhir Anand.
    — 1st ed.
    p. cm.
    Includes bibliographical references and index.
    ISBN: 0-9700929-4-6

    1. Hinduism. 2. Vedas. 3. Yoga. 4. Hinduism—Doctrines.
I. Title.
BL1202.A53 2000   294.5
                        QBI00-500130

Library of Congress Catalog Card Number: 00-191339

♻ *Printed in the United States of America on Recycled Paper*

294.5 ANA 2000
Anand, Sudhir.
The Essence of the Hindu
religion : with an

Satyam Eva Jayate

TRUTH ALWAYS ULTIMATELY PREVAILS

CONTENTS

PREFACE

The purpose of this book is to familiarize the reader with the essential beliefs of the Hindu religion and to provide an introduction to the philosophy and practice of yoga, which can direct one's life journey toward attaining God and bliss. The information presented in here is not the author's own interpretation of the Hindu religion, but rather it represents the message delivered by seers (sages) several thousand years ago in ancient India for the benefit of mankind.

There is considerable misrepresentation of many aspects of the Hindu religion in the West. It has been generally presented as a religion believing in multiple gods and worshipping animate and inanimate objects. There is the misconception that one can obtain salvation by chanting "secret mantras" and that one's fate is sealed at birth so one should passively accept his destiny. In part, these notions are correct when one superficially examines the rituals and practices of many Hindus, mostly because the spectrum of religious practices among Hindus, not unlike Christianity, varies quite a bit.

However, as this book will amply substantiate, the Hindu religion is the oldest monotheistic religion, and at the core Hindus believe in One God who is Almighty, the Master of the universe, Ultimate Protector and Universal Benefactor. Also, the Hindu religion is far from being passive; it is an action-oriented religion where our past and present deeds (called karma in Hindu scriptures) determine our own fate. God only judges our deeds and metes appropriate rewards.

The misrepresentation of Hindu religion, to a large extent, is the result of poor translation of ancient Hindu scriptures, which are all in Sanskrit. The Sanskrit used in the scriptures uses language, where a word often has more than one meaning. In addition, the scriptures contain the extensive use of symbolism or metaphors to clarify their true meaning so everyone from the learned to the unschooled can understand the message. However, if only a literal translation of the words of the scriptures is made, as has often been the case, then the meaning is very different from the original intent.

All Hindus, irrespective of the manner in which they practice the religion, acknowledge the Vedas[1] as the root source of their beliefs. The Vedas are a collection of about 20,000 hymns in Sanskrit called Mantras. They are believed to have been recorded by *rishis* (holy seers, yogis) following revelations in *samadhi*, the highest state of yoga: a superconscious state of meditation where God is eventually revealed. Samadhi is not a trance-like state as is usually described in English language dictionaries in the West. Hindus believe that the knowledge of the Vedas (having been revealed by God) is eternal and sacred, and their authority is considered final.

The *Vedic* (the word Vedic refers to Hindu scriptures called the Vedas) hymns were organized into four major branches: *Rig* (knowledge and science); *Saam* (devotion); *Yajur* (action); and *Atharva* (science) several thousand years ago in ancient India. They describe both spiritual and secular knowledge about God, soul, how to attain God and how to live a virtuous life, i.e., follow

---

[1]The word *veda* in ancient India was also sometimes added as a suffix to other fields of secular knowledge, e.g., Ayurveda. Ayurveda, which of late has become somewhat popular in the West as an alternate system of promoting good health, is not part of the regular four Vedas. Ayurveda is that branch of knowledge that promotes long life and good health and deals with disease cure as well. In its later origin, however, some of the information in Ayurveda is an extension of the knowledge in Rig and Atharva Veda. Understanding the basic message of the Vedas would greatly help one to understand the deeper message of Ayurveda.

dharma and what the relationship of humans with each other, community and society should be. They also provide knowledge about physical nature and the universe. All prayers in Vedas are to One God only and not to any other deity. The Vedas do not mention idol worship or praying before images of God. Later seers elaborated upon certain segments of the Vedas and these commentaries comprise the various Upanishads.

The emphasis in Yajur Veda is on proper deeds (karma), which explain how to live and work in this world to reach God and attain bliss. The last chapter (40th) of Yajur Veda contains 17 mantras that describe the gist of Yajur Veda, which is in fact, the essence of the Vedic Hindu religion. These mantras describe the attributes of God; they describe how humans should live on earth to progress in their lives and how to attain God and bliss. Because of the immense importance of these 17 mantras to Vedic Hindu belief, this chapter with minor modifications, was compiled into a separate Upanishad: *Ishopanishad* (also spelled *Eeshopanishad*). This book is a commentary on the 40th chapter of Yajur Veda to explain the essential beliefs of the Vedic Hindu religion.

Vedic Hindu religion is the oldest, continuous religion where the same prayer hymns are still sung to the same One God as they have been for thousands of years. Western scholars have often overlooked the fact that most Hindus, despite 600 to 800 years of Muslim rule and 200 years of Christian British rule, clung to their basic belief in God and teachings of the Vedas and Upanishads. This belief persisted despite Muslim rulers forcibly converting some Hindus to Islam and the aggressive proselytizing by European Christian missionaries with the British government's tacit approval.

Moreover, they maintained their basic belief in God and the Vedas despite the grossly corrupt teachings of the Hindu religion by the majority of the priestly class members. These people proved to be more interested in performing rituals to fleece the public and keep them ignorant, rather than impart the essential messages of the Hindu religion. Fortunately throughout this period, a few saintly persons did spread the true message of the Vedas through their words, devotion and deeds. These essential messages of the Hindu religion strongly influenced the common folks of India, along with the rituals propagated by the greedy priests. Although during that time, the majority of Hindus prayed and worshipped before deities of God, as well as idols of various gods and goddesses, these were usually considered symbolic representations of the many facets of the One Almighty God. Whereas, Christianity and Islam replaced and uprooted the older religions practiced in Rome, Europe, Egypt, Africa, the Middle East and the Americas, they had far less impact on the practice of Hindu religion.

Most Hindus did not (nor do they now) consider the One God of Christians to be different or superior to the One God they believed in and called OM or Brahman. Also, they did not (nor do they now) think that God's son Jesus was any different than their belief in much earlier incarnations of God in the form of Rama or Krishna. *Please note that Vedic Hindu religion does not acknowledge that God is ever born as a human being or will directly father a child. However, this does not prevent many Hindus from believing in God's incarnation as Rama or Krishna.*

Most Hindus did not (nor do they now) regard Christians praying before the Cross or to icons (idols) of Jesus Christ, Mary or other Christian patron saints any different from their own prayers before idols of Rama, Krishna or other Hindu gods or goddesses. Similarly, Hindus did not (nor do they now) deem Allah to be any different or superior to their belief in One God called Om or Brahman, nor did they find His special messenger Mohammed to have other characteristics than those of special messengers of God born in India.

The most famous teachings of Christ, especially those given at the Sermon on the Mount, which instruct people how to behave and how to revere God, are similar if not identical to those that had been stated a lot earlier in the Vedas and Upanishads.

Many teachings of Buddhism, especially the middle path in life and nirvana, have their origin in the Vedas and Upanishads. Buddha, after his enlightenment preached his sermons in India to reform the then prevailing malpractices within the Hindu religion, and only later did his followers spread his message to other parts of Asia including Southeast and Central Asia, China, Japan and Korea.

Yoga, which lately has become popular in the West, is an integral part of the Vedic Hindu religion. Yoga means union of soul with God. In the West, yoga has come to mean a collection of difficult stretching exercises, which often include contortions of the body, or it has meant meditation in a trance-like state. Exercises, however, are a very limited part of yoga. Yoga is a philosophical pursuit, which teaches spiritual, mental and physical discipline with the ultimate goal of attaining God and bliss.

This book presents the essential beliefs and principles of Hindu religion based on the Vedas and Vedic scriptures. Although opinions differ among Hindus as how to correctly interpret the Vedas, the author has followed the perspective espoused by Swami Dayanand Ji Saraswati and believes this to be the correct one.

This book does not focus upon the diverse practices and rituals of the Hindu religion. Some of the rituals, practices or their criticisms have been included at places, but only with limited descriptions, just to help the reader better understand the Hindu religion.

The book is divided into three sections. There is some degree of repetitive information in various sections; however, it is included because similar messages have been stated in different contexts and their re-inclusion can help one achieve a better understanding.

Section I: Basic Beliefs of the Hindu Religion

This section introduces some of the basic beliefs and concepts of the Hindu religion and the Hindu scriptures in general. It gives the proper definition of several important words, such as Om, Brahman, Dharma, Karma, Mantra and Guru. This introduction helps the reader understand the actual translation of Veda mantras included in this book, both in Section I and Section II.

Section II: 40th Chapter of Yajur Veda (Ishopanishad)

This section is devoted to translation of the 17 mantras of the 40th chapter of Yajur Veda. This includes a word-for-word translation (from Sanskrit to English) and also discusses the meaning and message of the mantra.

Section III: Introduction to Philosophy and Practice of Yoga

This section explains the philosophy of yoga and introduces the practice of eight steps of yoga for attaining God and finding bliss in life.

This book is a reaffirmation of the fact that through life's journey, an individual has the freedom to choose any path he or she wants; however, any deed a person performs in life has consequences, which depending upon each particular deed, may be good or bad.

The journey also has a purpose (unless one makes it aimless), which is to reach God and live a virtuous life where one has responsibilities not only to oneself but also to society.

I have written the book in plain English so that it would be useful to a lay person who is familiar with the Hindu religion only in a limited way. If the book helps anyone become a better person and/or find meaning in life, then the purpose of this book would be fulfilled.

The book is dedicated to honor Swami Dayanand Ji Saraswati, who about 150 years ago, re-introduced in India, the true message of the Vedas and other Hindu scriptures by translating them in simple language that the common people of India could understand. He also personally spent his life spreading that message. My goal in writing this book is to share the knowledge of the Vedic Hindu religion that I have learned from my mother Shrimati Sushila Anand and father Shri Jia Ram Anand; Pandit Harisharan Ji Sidhantalankar; Swami Omanand Ji Saraswati; Swami Satyam Ji; and other teachers. The book is dedicated to all of them, for they not only gave me the knowledge, but also with their own examples have shown me how to use this knowledge to make progress in life.

I want to acknowledge and extend my deepest gratitude to my friend Doctor Robert Christiansen in completing this book. Over the past nineteen years since we first met as colleagues at work, we have had innumerable fruitful discussions on many professional and secular subjects as well as religion. He has been extraordinarily helpful in critiquing the book and in improving the syntax and style. I am grateful for his assistance, encouragement and support.

I also want to give my deep thanks to my son Vikram Anand for his patience and generous help during the past several years to resolve the many computer glitches I encountered while completing this book, his critique and useful suggestions, as well as help with the cover design. Additionally, I want to extend my sincere thanks to my cousin Mrs. Jyoti Gandhi and her son Vikram Gandhi for their critique and helpful suggestions.

I also greatly appreciate the professional advice and help of Karen Stedman of PenMark Editorial Services and Christine Nolt of Cirrus Design.

> All profit from the sale of the book will be
> donated to various Vedic institutions to further spread
> the true message of Vedas and Yoga.

Section I

BASIC BELIEFS OF THE HINDU RELIGION

Since the beginning of time man has wanted to understand the meaning and purpose of life. He has been trying to answer such questions as: *what does it mean to be human; what is life all about; what is our purpose; is there a power higher than ourselves in the universe; is that Higher Power God; what is God like; do we have souls and, if so, what is the relationship of our souls to God?*

A group of very wise men called *rishis*, holy seers, considered these issues a long time ago in India; at the time they were in a state of *samadhi* (a superconscious state of enlightenment), which is the highest state that can be achieved through the practice of Yoga. In samadhi God directly reveals knowledge and wisdom to the soul. This knowledge was recorded in sacred texts, known as the Vedas, which form the basis of the Hindu religion.

This section begins with an introduction and a story about some of the basic beliefs of the Hindu religion. A detailed account of the meaning of the Sanskrit word for religion, *dharma*, will follow along with descriptions of the attributes of God, the soul and physical matter as viewed by the *Vedic* Hindu religion (the word *Vedic* refers to Hindu scriptures called the Vedas). This section will describe the main Hindu scriptures (such as the Vedas) and how they are organized. It also provides proper definitions of some important words such as *Hindu, Arya, karma, mantra* and *guru* and discusses the meaning and nature of prayer. Finally, some misconceptions about the Hindu religion commonly held both in India and in the West are explained, along with some of the reasons for these misinterpretations.

THE FOUR BASIC BELIEFS OF THE HINDU RELIGION

There are four fundamental beliefs in the Vedic Hindu religion that are essential to understand. These will be discussed briefly here and then explained in greater detail later on.

1. God: There is but One God. God alone is Almighty, the Supreme Power of the universe. God is the Universal Protector and Benefactor. God is everywhere. God is all-powerful and God knows everything: God is omnipresent, omnipotent and omniscient. God, however, is also far more than can be described by words alone and must be experienced within the soul. People call God different names: Hindus call God *OM, Brahman* or by other names; Jews refer to God as *Yahweh* and *Adonai*; Christians use the words *God* and *Lord* and Muslims the word *Allah*, but all these names refer to the very same God. (See pages 23–27, 77–80 and 92–94 for details on attributes of God).

2. Karma[1] (kur′mə, pronounced kurm): Karma means deed and every deed has consequences. Humans have free will and may perform any karma they choose. Judgement as to rewards or outcome of karma is solely in the hands of God. Good karma secures good rewards and bad karma produces misery. It is said, "As you sow, so shall you reap." Or "What goes around comes around." Both are expressions of the same truth. Sometimes the rewards of karma are almost instant: Putting your hand into a flame will yield almost immediate results. In other cases, however, the results may be delayed, perhaps even for a very long time. At times, it may seem that a person who performs good deeds is suffering (the product of previous bad karma), while a person committing sinful acts may appear to be doing well or to be happy (because of past good karma). However, a person's current bad

---

[1]The word karma implies **action** not fate. However, the word is often misused in the West in statements such as "This is my Karma" implying "this is my fate." Fate is the result (fruit) of the past karma. The results of past karma, which we bear, is called *bhoga* and not karma. All new karma is in the present and future.

deeds will not forever remain unpunished. The consequences of his actions will eventually have an effect. Ultimately, every karma has good or bad results depending on the nature of the act. The accumulation of good deeds brings us closer to God, peace and bliss both in this life and in the next in the form of rebirth on a higher spiritual plane of existence. The accrual of bad karma produces misery in this life and the next in that we will emerge as a lower life form, such as an animal or plant. This cycle of birth, death and rebirth will continue until the soul has attained *moksha* the infinite bliss (see below). (Also, see pages 28–33 and 80–87 for details on karma.)

3. *Moksha* (moksʹshə, pronounced Moksh): Moksha refers to attaining God and experiencing infinite bliss. The absolute goal of the soul is to find *moksha*. The means for attaining moksha is to live according to dharma (see below), practice meditation with faith and devotion, further one's spiritual knowledge and do selfless deeds. Together these things constitute the path of yoga. Over time, when these practices become so intense that a person totally devotes his or her life to seeking God and helping others and not doing any deeds for personal gratification, then the person's soul is liberated, or moksha is attained. When the soul achieves moksha it aligns itself with God. It does not merge with or become a part of God as some have said, but remains a separate entity and, after a very long time, may again be born as a spiritually endowed human being, such as rishis (holy seers, sages or wise men).

4. *Dharma*[1] (dhurʹmə, pronounced dhurm): Dharma refers to a moral or virtuous way of living. This path requires following moral principles in all aspects of one's life and includes a devotion to truth in thought, word and deed. It involves the practice of forgiveness, cultivating inner and outer purity, directing one's mind and senses towards virtuous deeds and away from sin, not

---

[1]The combined dh sound is a dental pronounciation and it does not exist in English. Hence, it is usually pronounced as a d as in "do" or "bed".

coveting those things that belong to others, reducing attachments to worldly things, controlling anger, and completing all actions in a thoughtful and patient manner. In addition, it is not enough to be content with one's own self-improvement; one must be generous and help others to improve their lives too. The dharma principles are based on teachings found in the Vedas and related scriptures. All Hindus are unified in acknowledging the Vedas as the basic source of their beliefs. The Vedas comprise a collection of about 20,000 mantras (hymns) written in Sanskrit, which are believed to have been revealed to rishis while in the state of samadhi and then written down. The Vedas describe both spiritual and secular knowledge to help people live according to God's principles (for details on dharma see pages 10–22 and for Vedas 41–44).

The following story captures the essence of the Vedic Hindu religion and serves as an excellent basis for understanding more detailed philosophical discussions that follow. There have been many versions of this story told over the years in India. The version recounted here is based on one of the oldest legends.

What Does God Do?: The Servant and the King

A long time ago there was a brave king who ruled in India and had many vassal kings in his empire. He was also prone to be interested in spiritual matters and would often have questions concerning God and the soul. One day he asked one of his senior counselors the following three questions:

1. Where does God live?
2. What does God do?
3. How does one find God?

He gave the counselor three days to answer these questions and further stipulated that the answers should be in terms that the common people in his kingdom could understand. During the three-day period, the counselor thought deeply about the questions and sought advice from other spiritual leaders as well.

Even so, he was not sure that the king would be satisfied with the replies that he had to offer.

His servant noticed that he was very upset and asked him what was wrong. The master tartly remarked that the king had given him the task of finding answers to three spiritual questions, and thus far he had failed to find satisfactory answers. When the servant offered to help, the counselor became irritated. Time was running out, and if the spiritual leaders could not help, it was ridiculous to think that a simple servant would be able to help. The servant finally convinced the counselor to reveal the three questions to him.

To the counselor's surprise the servant answered, "Master, do not be worried. I can answer the questions to the king's satisfaction." The counselor immediately demanded the answers, but the servant insisted that he would tell them only to the king. The counselor became furious with the servant and said to him, "You want to make a fool out of me by having me present an idiot such as you to the king to answer his questions." The servant replied, "Master, you may call me an idiot if you wish, but so far you have not found any appropriate answers to the questions and time is running out. I suggest that you tell the king that I can answer his questions to his satisfaction, and if I fail he can chop off my head for my audacity."

The counselor considered the situation for a moment and realized that there was no other solution to his predicament. He therefore agreed to present his servant to the king after admitting his own failure to find acceptable answers. The king was quite amused by the situation, but after some contemplation told the servant, "I am willing to listen to your answers since I realize that knowledge is not restricted to anointed leaders and master teachers. I want to remind you, however, that failure will be punished with decapitation. Please begin."

Question 1: Where does God live?

The servant requested a bowl of milk before answering the question. This was brought to him. The servant put his right index finger into the milk and twirled it around as though he was looking for something in the bowl. The king shouted at him, "What kind of foolishness is this? What are you doing?" The servant replied, "Your majesty, I am looking for butter." The king shouted, "You are a fool! Even a child knows that you cannot find butter in the milk by stirring it around with your finger. To get butter you must first separate the cream and then churn it."

The servant replied, "Your majesty, that is the answer to your first question. Just as the butter exists everywhere in the milk but you cannot see it until you properly process it, so God lives in every part of the universe even though you do not see Him with your eyes. God is everywhere. You cannot hide from God. God is omnipresent, both within you and outside of you. You do not have to go to the mountain top, into a cave or to a holy place to find God. Wherever you are that makes you think of God is holy, and He is there; eventually that becomes everywhere in the universe. You can find God while staying right here in your palace. I hope I have answered your first question to your satisfaction." The king was delighted because he had never heard such a simple yet elegant way of expressing the truth that God is everywhere.

Question 2: What does God do?

The servant asked the king if he posed the question as a student or as the ruler of the nation. The king humbly replied, "Though I am king of the country, I ask this question as a student." The servant then said, "Your majesty, we have an old tradition in India that whenever a student asks a question from a teacher (guru), the student honors the teacher by having the teacher sit in the more important seat." The king knew this tradition well, so he offered his throne to the servant while he himself took the servant's seat. The servant then replied, "Your majesty, this is just what God can do and often does. He can make kings out of servants and servants out of kings. We must all remember that our power on earth is transient. Great empires have come and gone, sometimes by being conquered by foreign foes and sometimes by internal decay and disintegration, and God sometimes causes their disruption with natural disasters. God is the Master of the universe and of all that is in it. God is the final Judge. As human beings we can control our karma but not its rewards. Based upon our karma, God metes out either rewards or punishments. As you sow, so shall you reap. God knows everything that happens in the universe, even our thoughts. No sinful deed can ever be hidden from God. Therefore, everyone should live righteously according to the dictates of dharma, and even a king is not exempt. He must always consider the welfare of his subjects his most important duty by placing it before his own wishes, desires and personal pleasures. We must always remember that God is Omnipotent and Omniscient." The king was delighted with the answer to his second question as well.

Question 3: How does one find God?

The servant answered, "Your majesty, you have already answered part of your own question when you said that you must properly process the milk in order to get butter from it. This is the way it is for us. To find God we must live according to the principles of dharma and perform deeds that uplift our souls and help our fellow human beings. God is perceived by our soul, not our eyes. The practice of yoga (meditation) with faith and devotion and the acquisition of knowledge from the Vedas will slowly but surely advance us toward God. Gradually, as our devotion to God becomes so focused that every moment of our life is used to seek God and help others, rather than living for personal pleasures, then shall we attain God."

The king was so overcome with joy at the answers the servant had given to his three questions that he made the servant his chief spiritual counselor.

The Meaning of the Word DHARMA

The word **religion** is the closest English translation for the Sanskrit word **dharma**. Dharma does not, however, signify belief in specific ideas (or dogmas) or participation in designated sacred prayers, rites or rituals on a regular (daily or weekly) schedule or on special occasions. More properly, dharma refers to a moral or virtuous way of living life with the eventual goal of knowing God and attaining bliss. This type of living is based on moral principles and includes moral commitments, moral duties, moral responsibilities and moral deeds or virtues that dharma declares are essential to every aspect of life. Thus, dharma helps one distinguish right from wrong or a good action from a bad one.

Dharma often does not represent the convenient or popular thing to do and may not reflect the majority opinion, but it is always the correct and moral thing to do. Concerning right and wrong, it has been said that a hundred wrongs do not make a right or that telling the same lie a hundred times does not make it the truth. While dharma may be based upon beliefs or knowledge, it always expresses its principles in the **act of living**. Therefore, dharma always requires active participation; there is no such thing as passive dharma. No one else can perform dharma for you. A priest may listen to your confession, accept your charitable donation and say prayers for you and make his living in this manner, but he cannot perform moral deeds on your behalf or buy your sins away. A further principle of dharma suggests that one must not only be content with one's own moral progress but must, as far as is feasible, help other fellow human beings to improve their lives as well.

There are two main definitions of dharma that have been quoted in India since ancient times. The first and more common one given by Manu (the first law giver of India) defines dharma as a combination of 10 virtuous acts (Manusmriti 6: 92). The other definition states that dharma is made up of all acts or deeds that help us proceed toward self-realization and the attainment of

God, peace and bliss both in this life and after death. This was first stated by Kannad rishi and is found in the *Vaisheshik Darshana* (1: 2–4).

Some of the 10 virtuous acts of dharma, according to Manu, are the same as or similar to the components of the first two steps of yoga (see pages 129–134). The two are intertwined: a person who is to become a true yogi (yoga master) must practice dharma. These 10 acts are classed as follows:

1. *Dhriti:* Thoughtfulness with patience and strength

All things in life, but particularly making important decisions, must be done after calm, considered and thoughtful analysis and never in an impulsive way. It is crucial to try to make wise decisions since they all have consequences. In dhriti, there is also an implied admonition not to commit self-destructive deeds. Even in the case of life and death or at other urgent times, it is one's previous experience with similar situations that will help one make a quick, yet thoughtful decision.

When a person is presented with a dilemma, counsel from wise persons may be very helpful. Further, once a sound decision has been reached, it is important to remain steadfast and not be swayed by people's critical, derogatory or threatening comments. The goal is not to please others but to have the patience, strength and courage to do the right thing. While there may be failures along the way, it is important not to become discouraged, but rather to try again. Dhriti does not imply passivity or being afraid to try something new if the results are unknown. It does, however, demand adequate planning before starting. Innovation is fine, but one must also think ahead and consider the effects of the innovation upon mankind and the physical universe. *"Think before you act."*

2. *Kshama:* Forgiveness

One must learn to forgive other people's mistakes. Forgiveness teaches us kindness and love toward others. It also shows us that all human beings are alike. Forgiveness reminds us that we could easily have made a similar mistake. It requires us to ask how we would like to be treated if the circumstances were reversed: would we want forgiveness or harsh punishment? Forgiveness is generally reserved for the unintentional harmful acts of others towards us as a result of ignorance or change of circumstances.

Intentionally harmful or criminal acts, on the other hand, always deserve appropriate punishment by people in authority to deter others from similar actions. If one wishes to "turn the other cheek" and forgive someone else's intentional acts, that personal choice is always possible. This kind of saintly behavior however, is not expected from everyone, including the government authorities. God is immensely forgiving and kind, but God also is just and punishes sinners. *"To err is human, to forgive divine."*

3. *Dama:* **Mental discipline**[1]

4. *Indriya Nigrah:* **Controlling the sensory and action (motor) organs**

These two are discussed together as they are interrelated. It is important to learn to discipline the mind to concentrate upon important tasks, especially those at hand, and not allow the mind to wander aimlessly seizing upon whatever presents itself. The mind is curious; its nature is to flit from one thought to another regardless of whether the thought is serious or frivolous, good or bad. The goal is to channel the mind to think good and positive thoughts both towards oneself and others. A major way to achieve this is to reduce material or worldly desires. Disciplining the mind is crucial to both meditation and to the attainment of bliss (see the section on yoga for details). An undisciplined and wandering mind will only build castles in the air and may conceive of harmful and destructive acts toward oneself or others.

The information the mind obtains about the outside world is received through our sensory (or perception) organs. It is

---

[1] For various aspects of the mind as used in Vedic scriptures, e.g., *Mana, Chit, Budhi,* and *Ahankara,* see pages 118–125 in Section III, Yoga.

processed and the response occurs via the action (motor) organs. In the Vedas, Upanishads and Yoga scriptures the mind is considered to be the controller of the senses. In one of the Upanishads, called Kathopanishad, the human body is compared to an excellent chariot, the senses to powerful horses, the mind to reins, the intellect to a skilled charioteer and the soul to the owner, who via the charioteer and the reins, guides the direction the horses should take (Kathopanishad 3: 3–6). One would certainly want strong and powerful horses instead of weak ones, but one would also want them to be properly controlled rather than run amuck. Similarly, one should aim at having sharp and strong senses, but they must be directed by the soul via the mind to the right direction, instead seeking wild enjoyment of sensory pleasures without regard to the consequences.

The five sensory (perception) organs and their respective senses are as follows:

Ears:	hearing, listening
Eyes:	seeing, visualizing
Skin:	touch
Tongue:	taste
Nose:	smell

The five action (motor) organs and their responses are as follows:

Mouth:	speaking, eating
Arms:	performing tasks
Legs:	moving, walking, running
Sex organs:	procreating, having sexual intercourse
Excretory organs:	urinating, defecating

The five sensory organs are always sending new information to the mind from the outside world. It is possible, though, to have a certain degree of control over those things that are allowed to stimulate the sensory organs. One may choose to read a spiritual story or a racy novel, listen to uplifting music or a trashy pop-culture song, eat well and in moderation or overindulge on junk foods. It is also possible to choose whether to respond to other people each day with kindness or cruelty. The emphasis in the Vedic religion has always been upon controlling sensory input because when this is done, it is easier to rein in the action organs.

The mind can also have sensory or motor experiences from past memories, such as visualizing objects or persons with the eyes closed or hearing music that is merely thought of. In Vedic scriptures this is considered to result from the activation of *subtle inner senses* that directly interact with the mind. From past experiences, the mind has developed an extensive repertory of both sensory inputs and action responses. Disciplining the mind becomes a matter of using introspection or self-analysis, of focusing or concentrating the mind and continually directing it to stay on the right path.

Once the sensory organs have been properly trained to bring better messages to the mind, and the action organs are trained to respond in a more disciplined fashion, then concentrating and channeling the mind toward meditation becomes much easier. *"Think good thoughts." "See no evil, hear no evil, speak no evil, do no evil."*

5. *Shouch:* Cleanliness, purity

Shouch refers to being pure and clean both inside and outside. External environmental cleanliness and peace and quiet are essential for physical and mental well-being. Inner cleanliness is even more important. It requires self-examination, the acknowledgement of bad habits and their correction, overcoming pride, greed, lust, anger, jealousy, envy and laziness and acquiring honesty and integrity.

God is always pure and radiant, but the soul may often be obscured by impurities. It is only when these impurities are washed away that the soul may know itself and God and achieve bliss. Manu said that the body is cleansed by water, the mind by truth and the soul by austerity, self-reflection and spiritual knowledge (Manusmirti 5:109). *"Cleanliness of mind is next to godliness."*

6. *Asteya:* Not coveting

The common meaning given to asteya is simply, "Do not steal what belongs to others." This is punishable by law in most countries and cultures. A deeper, more important meaning however, forbids the coveting of another's property for any reason. Overcoming the mind's desire for that which belongs to others is much more difficult than overcoming the act of physical theft. The first step involves learning to be content with what one has that was earned by honest effort and hard work. Equally important is learning to reduce one's desires and to acquire only what one needs rather than what one wants. Reducing desires makes contentment a lot easier to achieve than when wants are many. It is important to become grateful for what one has and to learn to become generous and share with others, especially those less fortunate (see pages 77–80). *"Do not covet what belongs to others."*

7. *Akrodh:* Overcoming anger

Anger is a terrible vice that may cause even reasonable people to lose all sense of logical thinking and perform acts that at most times would be unthinkable. Anger provokes the tendency to be cruel rather than to be kind and non-violent. During a fit of anger, whether or not the angry person succeeds in harming the other party, he harms himself the most. Anger also creates unhappiness. Overcoming anger eventually makes people happy and cheerful and improves physical and spiritual well-being. Conquering anger does not mean suppressing it, as it will smolder and then burst forth later on. Some popular psychology recommends that one "get the anger out." Although this may make the person feel better for a moment, it rarely deals with the effects of anger on the inner-self and the other party.

The Vedic Hindu religion points out that anger is always self-destructive and will persist until one understands the reasons for the anger and deals with the root problem. The major causes for anger include the inability to fulfill one's desires (right or wrong), jealousy, vanity and pure blind ego. Ways to reduce anger include reducing desires and wants and learning to think of other people's needs as well as one's own. *"Anger burns from inside and provokes cruelty."*

8. *Vidya* (vid'yä): **Knowledge**

The Vedic religion considers knowledge far more important than money or material treasures. Knowledge is that kind of treasure that thieves cannot steal, and yet, requires no guards to protect it. The more one gives it away, the more it increases for the giver. The only caveat is that knowledge be transferred to a deserving person rather than to someone who will use it for evil or exploitative purposes. According to the Vedas and the Upanishads, there are two types of knowledge, *vidya*—spiritual knowledge, and *avidya*—knowledge of the material world and physical universe. (*Avidya* in theVedas and Upanishads *generally* does not mean ignorance, although it has been often mistranslated in this fashion.) Both types of knowledge have their benefits. Avidya is useful in finding a vocation or in better understanding the material world and the physical universe; and vidya would be beneficial in progressing toward God and attaining bliss (see pages 99–101 for further details). Moreover, knowledge exists at two levels, superficial and deep. Superficial knowledge involves memorizing a lot of information that can be acquired through books about secular and/or spiritual subjects without attaining a personal positive impact. Deep or discriminative knowledge, called *viveka*, enlightens a person allowing him to see things as they really are and to follow truth and virtue in life. *"Vidya is a better treasure than wealth."*

9. *Dhee:* **Intellect to discriminate right from wrong**

According to the Vedic scriptures, the ability of the mind to think, analyze and make judgments is divided into four types, which are, in ascending order of merit: *Buddhi, Dhee, Medha* and *Prajna.* (For medha and prajna see page 122 in Yoga: Section III.)

a. Buddhi: This is the usual or ordinary level of intelligence that most humans possess. It is the process of thinking that allows us to function in our daily lives. A person who lacks sufficient buddhi is said to be retarded, and one with deranged buddhi is considered insane. Buddhi, based upon previous experiences, helps us decide such things as when to fight and when to flee, whether things appear right or wrong or whom to trust and whom not to. One component of buddhi is instinct or gut feeling. Instinct is not unique to humans since animals also possess it, but as far as we know, they lack the ability to think.

b. Dhee: This refers to intellect with the power to discriminate and separate right from wrong, truth from falsehood and propaganda from correct information. It also helps one understand moral responsibility and the need to act accordingly. Dhee is the intellect that helps a person follow the path of virtue even when tempted to do otherwise. A Hindu novice starting on his spiritual journey will traditionally be told to begin by praying for *dhee* or *dhiya*. Not until dhee has been acquired can one progress in yoga to the higher levels of buddhi called medha and prajna. **Without being able to discriminate between right and wrong a person is less than human.**

10. *Satya* (sut'yə): Truth

Truth is the value that transcends all other moral values. Truth is the foundation on which all human interaction is based. Even liars use the pretense of truth in their dealings with others. It is necessary to always be willing to accept that which is true and discard that which is not in every aspect of life. To be scrupulously honest may require giving up financial or personal security or social position. Discarding cherished beliefs may be necessary, and in the final analysis, sacrificing one s life too. Because of the fear of giving up their security or beliefs, most people at times are willing to lie. Also, they are more afraid of getting caught in a lie than actually lying. The inner joy and strength that a completely honest person feels can never be experienced by a liar.

Truth in the Vedic Hindu religion is considered at three levels:

a. Thought	mental	intent
b. Word	verbal	expression
c. Deed	action	execution

It is important to make a diligent effort to adhere to the truth in thought, word and deed. One Veda Mantra states: "Your inside should be the same as what you state outside" (Atharva Veda 2: 30: 4). When a person says the right words, but the action betrays the words, it's a deception. Because of this people are judged by what they do rather than by what they say. Many politicians and lawyers and other people in society are particularly adept at such deceptions. It is important to speak clearly to be easily understood and then to have the courage to carry out what you say (Rig Veda 4: 33:6). Once one really starts to follow the truth, thoughts of lying or not carrying out a promised action permanently end.

God is considered the Eternal and Ultimate Truth in the Vedas and Upanishads and truth is frequently emphasized as the most important aspect of dharma (religion).

There is no reason for a discrepancy between religion and science in the pursuit of truth. These two are not incompatible because they pursue the truth from different vantage points. While the scientific pursuit of truth is highly commendatory, the concept of truth originated in the pursuit of basic human moral values. The perception of what is true in science continues to change as more knowledge is made available. Once it was believed that the atom was the basic unit of the universe and that it could not be split further or converted into another form, such as energy. These "truths" have changed over time. On the other hand, moral truth, particularly God's truth, is eternal and never varies. Through its method of physical observation, modern science can neither prove nor disprove the existence of God. The existence of God can only be perceived by the soul through the practice of spiritual science of meditation (yoga). ***Truth always ultimately prevails.***

The definition of dharma as contained in the 10 principles just described consists of universal principles and values that are not the exclusive property of any specific religion or sect. Other virtues such as effort, perseverance, generosity, charity, selfless giving, compassion, non-violence, austerity, honesty, integrity and faith are all implied in the 10 principles and are mentioned in the Vedas and many other Vedic Hindu scriptures.

Dharma does not consist in simply knowing the words attached to the principles, but instead is the act of adopting them in one's personal life and making the best effort possible to live by them. Following the path of dharma may be quite difficult at the outset and may feel lonely because those close to you may choose to do otherwise. Once there exists the intention of incorporating dharma into one's life, then the pursuit of truth and faith in God become one's closest companions and provide the inner strength required to move forward. Living according to dharma now becomes one's inner conscience, and one speaks the truth not because of fear of being caught lying but because it is the right thing to do.

The initial progress might seem a bit slow as it is often necessary to unlearn previous bad habits, but the journey is ultimately worth the effort. The practice of dharma requires constant effort and vigilance because there are many distractions along the way, such as the pursuit of money, fame, power, sex, amusement or other indulgences. Only a person, who conquers these distractions and remains steadfast through all the trials, has the right to be called a religious person. Such persons experience increasing inner joy, peace and spiritual strength as they progress along the road to God.

While Hindus who are aware of all or some of these principles of dharma, understand that they will eventually lead to knowing God, few Hindus actually practice **all** the principles. Most Hindus, like other "religious" people, will pick and choose, incorporating some of the principles to varying degrees in their daily lives but otherwise continue on as they always have. Most Hindus (like others) spend most of their effort trying to enjoy whatever worldly pleasures they can obtain and continue to struggle with the personal and/or financial shortcomings of life rather than pursue the path of dharma. Others will pay lip service to dharma, but when problems arise they want quick and easy solutions that require minimal effort and very little change in their manner of living. This "quick fix" explains the desire to look for miracles. It is important to remember that no significant results will come from limited effort and that miracles are few and far between. Most people will find excuses or rationalize the way they live their lives, rather than go through the effort of pursuing virtue. Such rationalizations will eventually produce feelings of emptiness and lack of purpose and create anxieties over the uncertainties of life and the absence of peace, happiness and freedom.

In the *Bhagavad Gita* master-yogi (*Yogiraj*) Krishna explains to Arjuna that among all the people in the world, there are only a few who are really interested in the spiritual aspects of life. And among those there are only a very small number who actually pursue the religious path in earnest (Gita 2: 29). Nevertheless, those who do pursue such a path and lead a spiritual life will find inner peace and joy and will ultimately attain bliss.

The following story is often told in India to explain the difference between rote knowledge versus true learning in living according to the principles of dharma.

ALWAYS FOLLOW THE TRUTH:[1]

The Teacher and the Pupil

A long time ago there was a famous guru who taught many students. One day it happened that the teacher taught a lesson

---

[1]This story is often attributed to the *Mahabharata;* however, the story does not exist anywhere in the *Mahabharata*. The original source of the story is unknown.

about always adhering to the truth. The following day he gave his students a test on the lesson. Most of the students could remember and recite the main points, but a few failed. The next day the teacher tested those who had failed the day before. All the students but one passed. The teacher became very angry with the lone student that failed and screamed at him, "You fool! Why can't you remember this simple lesson? What is the matter with you? You used to be a good student."

The student politely replied, "Sir, I am trying, but I keep failing." This same scenario repeated itself for four more days, and each day the teacher not only became angrier but also more and more perplexed because the student behaved normally and nothing seemed to be wrong with him. On the seventh day, the student returned and told the teacher, "Sir, yesterday was the first day in my life when I do not recall telling even a single lie to anyone." The teacher's eyes overflowed with tears as he hugged the student and said, "Son, I apologize to you for all my anger. I had lost the ability to recognize the difference between plain rote memory and real learning where the student must practice what he learns. Son, you alone in the whole class have learned the lesson while all the others failed! May God bless you that from now on you always speak the truth."

This story shows that adopting the principles of virtuous living is true dharma as opposed to merely reciting them. The true test of a person's virtue is revealed when he or she is faced with temptation and chooses the path of dharma rather than the softer, easier way of temptation.

After a while when following dharma becomes a way of life, God is one's friend and companion, and the approval of others is not necessary. The inner joy, strength and courage that this brings make the effort far easier. While there may be slips and failures, it is important not to lose courage. All one needs to do is to learn from mistakes and go forward without repeating them.

There is no especially favorable time in life to start following the path of virtue. The time to begin is now. Every day and every moment is new and has the blessing of God. As the Chinese proverb says, "The journey of a thousand miles begins with but a single step." Eventually a person will know God and experience bliss if he continues to make the effort. His faith, devotion, perseverance to stay on the right path and avoid distractions will aid in his progress.

All that has been discussed up to this point refers to the observance of the principles of dharma in personal daily life. If everyone in the entire society lived by these rules, there would be peace and happiness on earth. But because not everyone in a society chooses to live by the principles of dharma, it's necessary for the government to make rules or laws that define dharma (moral conduct of life) at a minimal level in order to allow society to function. Those who break these laws are punished.

The government should not require that its citizens follow the principles of dharma since that is a personal decision. The government has no right to interfere, except as individual behavior impacts upon the rights or freedoms of others. In any case, it would be impossible to enforce personal laws, such as a law that forbids coveting others' goods, because the government cannot patrol people's minds. Good personal conduct always represents a standard that is higher than the ones prescribed by law.

THE ETERNAL IN THE HINDU RELIGION

According to the Vedas (the basis of Hindu belief), there are three things that are eternal: *God*, the *Soul* and *Prakriti* (*Physical Matter or Universe*). The attributes of these three are as follows:

God is Sat-Chit-Anand (Sachidanand):
Sat = the eternal, truth
Chit = conscious, alive
Anand = all bliss

Soul is Sat-Chit
Sat = the eternal, truth
Chit = conscious, alive

Prakriti (Physical Matter or Universe) is only Sat
Sat = the eternal, truth

THE ATTRIBUTES OF GOD

God is *omnipotent*: He is the Master of the universe with all its riches. God alone is Almighty, the Ultimate Protector and Universal Benefactor. God is the Highest Power and the Supreme Force. God is the ultimate source of all activity in the universe. Because God is eternal, He was never born, and thus, will never die. He is the Supreme Consciousness. God is the Reality that never changes. God is *omnipresent:* He has neither shape nor form, yet is present everywhere, permeating every part of the universe from that which is nearest to us to that which is farthest away. There is no need to travel to "holy" places to find God, for He is right here, within us and around us. God is *omniscient:* He knows everything that happens in the entire universe even the merest detail and yet is also the master of all spiritual and secular knowledge based upon truth. God is kind, but He is also just. God is the source of all bliss—He is Supreme Bliss.

God has many more attributes and has been given hundreds of names in both the Vedas and the Upanishads. Some of these attributes have been often mistakenly translated as the names of specific deities. Nevertheless, the Vedas maintain that there is One God and only One God. (See pages 77–80 and 92–94 for further information on the many attributes of God.)

In the Vedas the oneness of God is described as follows: *Aikum Sat Vipra Bahuda Vadanti* (Rigveda 1: 164: 46 and Atharvaveda 9: 10: 28).

Aikum	*Sat*	*Vipra*
The One and Only God	exists eternally	wise persons

Vadanti	*Bahuda*
have called God	by many names.

The One God of the Hindus called Om or Brahman is the same as the One God called Yahweh by the Jews, God or Lord by the Christians or Allah by the Muslims. The following two examples are sometimes quoted in India to explain the Oneness of God and the reason why He has so many names:

There is only one thing in the world that we know by the name water, but water is often called by different names depending upon its physical state and locality. When frozen it is called ice. When ice covers a large area in a river or sea, it is called glacier, icecap or iceberg. Water can also be in the form of rain, snow, sleet, hail, slush, or dew. Water can be contained in a well, a spring, a creek, a reservoir, a pool, a pond, a lake, a brook, a stream, a river, a bay, an ocean or the sea. It can be as fine as a light mist, appear as a burst of steam or be relentless and fierce during a monsoon.

When water from one source is mixed with water from another source, it's not possible to separate the sources because it just blends together as water. So too, there is only One God and even though He is called so many different names, He remains the same One God.

The second illustration uses the names given to one person. Say, for example, someone is named Ram. He might be called son by his parents, husband or spouse by his wife, father by his children, grandfather by his grandchildren, brother by his siblings, friend by his friends, mentor by his students and so on but he is just one person with different names or descriptions.

OM is the name in the Hindu religion that is reserved for God alone. Even those who believe in a various deities, gods and goddesses have never named any one of them Om. Om is represented by the symbol ॐ; it is composed of three vowel sounds without a consonant:

A is pronounced like the sound of "u" in but ⎤ The sounds A
U is pronounced like the sound of "u" in put ⎦ and U together
                                                   are pronounced
M is hummed like the "m" in hu<u>mmmm</u> and   as O
    not as consonant sound eM

These three sounds represent the fact that God is the Ultimate Protector and Universal Benefactor, and that God is *omnipresent*, *omnipotent* and *omniscient* as well as having many other attributes such as Sat-Chit-Anand described earlier. The attributes of God that can be described in words are called *Saguna*. Om/God is also, however, outside what words alone can describe (the aspects of God which are beyond description are called *Nirguna*) and must be perceived by the soul through meditation (yoga).

BRAHMAN (brəhmən) is another name for God alone and is not to be confused with words Brahma or Brahmin (brä′hmin) (page 37). Brahman exists in two different states. *Shudh Brahman* (pure Brahman) is where God is a manifestation of the Supreme Consciousness, having all knowledge and all power but His creative energy is inactive. Thus, quietness, calm, peacefulness and purity are everywhere. During this state all physical matter is in its primal state and all souls are out of body and at peace. *Shabal Brahman* occurs when God's creative energy is activated to form the manifest universe. In this state of creation *Shabal Brahman* is called Brahma. It is at this time God establishes the unchanging rules for the existence of the universe and for the souls that occupy it. And, even God does not deviate from these rules. For instance, God would not perform unusual miracles, such as making the sun rise in the west or turning fish into humans. He would not be born as a human being or have a son, although many Hindus believe that God was born as Krishna or Rama, just as Christians believe that Jesus was the son of God. All these acts are against God's rules. While maintaining the universe, Brahman is called Vishnu. When the cycle of the universe is over, God directs the dissolution of the universe back into its primal material state. This destructive form of Brahman is called Mahesh or sometimes Rudra or Shiva.[1] This trinity of different "Gods or gods" (Brahma, Vishnu and Shiva), which has been incorrectly described by Western scholars as three separate deities of the Hindu religion, are actually three aspects of the same One and Only God.

God is the judge of all our thoughts and deeds. He will mete out the appropriate rewards and punishments according to our deeds and the motivations behind them. Some of these rewards and punishments are immediate, while others may take a long time to manifest. They may appear sometime in our current life or later on in a future life. (See attributes of soul for details.)

God in His immense kindness is the inner voice to our soul and is constantly giving us enlightenment and inspiration to lead us on the correct path and to do the right thing. The inner joy that we feel when we do the right thing comes from God. When we are following the right path, despite pressures and temptations to do otherwise, we will hear God's voice (our inner voice) speak to us and inspire us. Similarly, when we think evil thoughts or plan to do something wrong (lying, stealing, hate) God creates an aversion in us toward such thoughts and behavior. The reason people fail to follow the right course and commit a wrong or sometimes even heinous acts is that they have ceased listening to God's voice. The more we ignore this inner voice the less we will hear it, even though God's voice is always present. People who act as though they have no conscience can be are regarded as no longer behaving like humans. They may be considered subhuman in this life, and

---

[1]Although the word Shiva has usually been connected with the destructive ability of God, it actually means the Benefactor who showers us with His blessings.

in the next life they will further reap the consequences of their actions.

Generally, people do not think much about God when things are going relatively well. It is only when significant disappointments or major problems arise despite one's best efforts that people cry out to God for help. Many people will say such things as, "Why me?" or "God, please help me."

Some people eventually realize that they cannot control many of the events in their lives as some of their best laid plans can be suddenly and radically altered by such calamities as an earthquake, flood or fire. Lightening may even strike someone nearby and spare them, and this is when they turn to God realizing that a Higher Power is truly in control.

In contrast, many non-believers state boldly that God does not exist in the 21st (until last year 20th) century, and with advances in science God will become eventually obsolete. When asked why some people are lucky and others unlucky, these people usually state that this is random and not a result of divine direction. However, many will often add that they do not understand the vagaries of statistical chance; thus, they may perhaps acknowledge in a small way the existence of a Higher Power.

THE ATTRIBUTES OF THE SOUL

In the Vedas and Hindu scriptures the SOUL is most frequently called *Atma* (ät'mä), but also has several other names. While there is only one God, there are many souls. Like God, the soul is eternal and has conscious energy, but its energy is very limited when compared to God. A major difference between God and the soul is that only God is bliss; souls do not have bliss. Despite such limitations, however, the individual soul can be enlightened by living according to dharma, practicing yoga and being devoted to God and indeed may ultimately experience bliss—attain moksha.

All living things have souls. Soul is the principle of life. It is the possession of a soul that differentiates living things from inanimate objects or physical matter. The main forms of life according to the Vedas and other Hindu scriptures are: (1) humans (*manav, manushya*); (2) animals (*jangam—mobile life forms*); and (3) plants (*sathawar—immobile life forms usually rooted in the ground*).

In humans, the soul is the ultimate center of all learning (thought and knowledge); feelings (happiness or suffering); and karma (actions or deeds). Only human souls are considered to have free will and carry the responsibility for their actions (karma). Even though the individual has free will, once an act is performed it is God alone who judges and administers justice. While children are responsible for their actions in only a limited way, the adult has free will and is fully responsible for his or her actions. The decision as to what kind of deeds to perform and therefore whether to move closer to or away from God resides with the individual. This means that part of growing up is to shoulder this responsibility and not to blame one's parents, friends or others for one's actions. (See below and pages 80–87 for more on karma.)

Human beings may be assigned to four different classes depending upon personal characteristics and type of deeds performed.

- *Deva* contains those who are always doing good for mankind and the universe. They are the embodiment of virtue or dharma. They are generous persons; they give to others without expecting anything in return. People such as they deserve honor and respect and are considered godly or saintly persons. In the Hindu religion, physical objects and forces, such as the sun, the earth, air, water and fire have often been called deva because of their helpfulness to mankind; and some Hindus have considered them objects of worship. Deva is also another name for God and is called this in many Veda Mantras.

- *Pitri* comprises those nurturing people who are helpful to others. Overall, they are considered mostly good. They give to others, but ask for something in return. Good (nurturing) parents generally fit into this class. The Sanskrit word *pitri* has the same root as the English word "paternal."

- *Manushya* embodies the average person who is a mixture of both good and bad. They are mostly self-centered but do not harm others in achieving their goals. They are usually the average, normal-type people.

- *Asura* refers to those who are mostly bad but may have some good traits. They are generally unjust, selfish, envious of others, untruthful, often lazy and deceptive and try to gain rewards through any means possible but without honest effort. They may be very bright and knowledgeable. They may also be aware or understand the concept of dharma, but they do not incorporate it into their lives. These people also never do their share of the work but are always ready to demand more than their fair share of the rewards. The worst members of this class are called *Rakshasa* and *Pishacha*, and they are parasites on society. Their deceptiveness causes them to talk of goodness, and they may fool people for a time, but their basic nature is eventually revealed.

As human beings, we are all at different stages of our development and contain both good and bad elements from our karmas generated in this as well as previous lives. The idea is not to indulge in self-pity because of one's circumstances but to strive to become better by living a righteous life and doing virtuous deeds. Improvement is a slow process and sudden transformations are unusual, but if there is consistent effort progress is certain. And, the greater the effort, the greater the progress. Because of free will, each person has the capacity to perform better karma in the present and future, so there is always hope for future spiritual advancement.

As social beings, we have love and affection for our parents, spouses, children, other family members and friends. We also have responsibilities to our families, friends and society at large, and the Vedas encourage us to fulfill them with love, affection and vigor. But we are not to make this love and affection a type of bondage over others. The Vedas suggest that we liberate ourselves as well as help liberate others to follow their own respective paths in life. It is important to remember that all these human relationships are transitory and that only our relationship to God is permanent. Eventually family relationships should be expanded to include the whole society. In order to overcome the emotional attachments that result in our soul's bondage, it is necessary to do selfless work in the service of God and to learn to acquire love for everyone in the universe. Living this way is not easy for most people, and only a select few choose this path. Nevertheless, this is the path that helps one become a *deva* person and eventually attain *moksha*.

Devas and Asuras: who is better?

The following story is often told in India to illustrate the differences between deva and asura behavior.

At one time there was a quarrel between the Asuras and the Devas as to whose value system was better: Was it was better to be selfish and self-centered or to be interested in the welfare of others in addition to one's own?

They all traveled to Prajapati (master of everyone in the universe) to ask his opinion. Prajapati began by replying, "All of you have traveled most of the morning to come here and must be hungry by now. Therefore, I want all of you to be my guests and first have lunch, and then in an hour I will give you my opinion." Prajapati's courtiers served the same excellent lunch to both the Devas and the Asuras but in separate dining halls.

Before lunch could begin Prajapati told both parties, "There is one condition I have before you start eating. My courtiers will tie arm-boards behind both elbows so that you will not be able to bend your elbows while you eat. Enjoy your meal!" Now in the first hall every Asuras' mouth was watering at the sight of the delicious food, but no one could figure how to get the food into his mouth. They tried to eat by tossing up the food in the air and by attempting to catch it in their mouths. An occasional morsel of food would fall into someone's mouth, but most of the food fell onto the floor and onto his or her clothes. The place was a mess and most of the Asuras were cursing Prajapati, calling him a practical joker and accusing him of torturing his hungry guests.

Meanwhile, in the other hall, the Devas also could not bend their elbows to put the food into their mouths. But they quickly realized that they could feed the person sitting opposite them at the table even though they could not feed themselves. Thus, the pairs fed one another and everyone enjoyed the feast. At the end of the hour Prajapati reappeared and asked if all had enjoyed the meal. The Asuras snidely told Parajapati that he had played a mean joke on them, while the Devas said that the meal was both enjoyable and delicious. Prajapati of course knew all this for he had been watching the parties and then told the Asuras how the Devas had managed to have such an excellent feast and why the Devas' value system was better than theirs. He said that it is never good to be selfish and content solely with one's own progress; for it is in assisting others that we all achieve our goals.

In the Vedas and other Hindu scriptures there is much emphasis on being generous and giving to others (Rig Veda 1: 29: 4; Rig Veda 10: 117: 6; Atharva Veda 3: 24: 5; and 20: 74: 4). In Sanskrit, giving (charity) is called *daan* (or *daanum*), and it is usually grouped into three categories called *tana, mana* and *dhana*. Tana is giving in the form of bodily or physical service. Mana is giving at mental or word level and dhana is monetary or material giving. All three types of giving are praiseworthy and noble, and depending upon the circumstances, one may be more important than the others. The most difficult form though, is selfless (volunteer) service at the physical level. An example would be to tend to the physical needs of an invalid person unknown to you or to bring food to the hungry. The next level of selfless giving is to provide mental support, such as counseling or encouraging someone, giving a lecture or writing a book to inspire others or promote virtue. The last level is donating money or gifts to charitable organizations so that others can take care of people's needs is the easiest of the three types of donations, even though in most societies, it receives the most recognition. A few caveats about giving (charity) include: Give only to deserving people or causes in a selfless manner with no desire for fame or recognition. And, donations of ill gotten money to atone for one's sins is not virtuous.

In contrast to humans, in every other life form the soul is considered to be bound rather than free. Non-human forms are living but bear the consequences of deeds performed in previous lives. Animals are not responsible for their actions. They act out of instinct, rather than by free will; therefore, these actions do not carry consequences for the future of the soul. Animals are merely passing time doing penance for the past deeds of the soul while it was in human form with a free will.

The soul is eternal. It does not die with the death of the physical body. In the *Bhagavad Gita*, Krishna says, "Soul is eternal, weapons can not harm it, fire can not burn it, and at so called death it only changes the physical form surrounding it." (*Gita* 2: 23, 24.) Each time the soul enters a new physical body it is like a person who changes into new clothes (*Gita* 2: 20–22).

In the *Kathopanishad*, Yamacharya gives a similar teaching to Nichiketa (*Kathopanishad* 2: 18–19). At the death of the physical body the soul is reborn many times depending on past deeds until it attains God (*moksha*) and is liberated. The soul itself is always pure, but it is coated over by all our worldly attachments and the results of our past deeds. It is only after we have removed all of the covering layers by following dharma, doing virtuous deeds, helping others and practicing meditation (yoga) that we can come to the pure soul, which is the only one that can attain God and find bliss. Gradually as our devotion to God becomes so focused that every moment our life is spent in seeking God and acting in God's service, then all bondages of the soul are liberated, and we attain God and moksha.

As stated before, this is the ultimate goal of the soul, to attain moksha. In this state, the soul remains constantly close to God and is one with God but does not become God. Such a soul after a very very long period of time is reborn as a highly spiritually endowed human being. Having been born again though, the soul is nevertheless subject to all the rules and conditions that apply to all human beings.

It is important to mention that in India another school of thought exists that believes God and the soul are the very same Supreme Consciousness and not separate entities. It is only that the soul is a small segment of the Supreme Consciousness and is seeking to reunite with it. Such believers are considered non-dualists (or monoists) and follow the doctrines of Shankaracharya (a great Indian scholar, who by some accounts lived about 1,200 years and by others 2,400 years ago). At present, this belief is accepted by several Hindu organizations in India and by some in the West such as the Vedanta Society. The non-dualists believe that at the time of liberation, the soul realizes it is same as God, merges completely with God and is never reborn. Some non-dualists also believe that soul is not responsible for the performance of karma, but instead is a silent witness to the actions of the body and mind. As stated before, the Vedas and the Upanishads clearly identify three separate entities: God, soul and matter. In the Upanishads a liberated soul has been described as attaining bliss (moksha) but it neither becomes Supreme Bliss nor achieves the other attributes of God. At times, such as soul has been called *Eeshwar* or *Ishwara* (a name also used for God) but is never called *Parameshwar* (the Supreme Master) a name reserved only for God. Soul may be called *Atma* or *Jivatma* but never *Paramatma* (Supreme Soul).

THE ATTRIBUTES OF PRAKRITI (PHYSICAL MATTER)

Physical matter (*prakriti:* pruk'ritë) is also eternal but has neither conscious energy nor bestows bliss because it is innately inert. From time to time, physical matter is either activated and transformed by God's creative power into the manifest universe as we know it (*srishti*), or inactivated and dissolved (*pralaya*) back into its dormant primal state (Rig Veda 10: 190: 1–3). A single cycle of activation and dissolution of the universe is referred to as Brahma's One Day. Such cycles of creation and dissolution go on forever in an infinite series of universes. The energy needed for the constant motion of the universe (movement of the planets, stars and galaxies as well as the movement of water and wind on the earth) is not spontaneous but was provided by God at the beginning of each creation (the equivalent of *Big Bang*). God is the Master Architect and the Power that maintains order in the universe.

All nonliving objects, as well as physical bodies of all living things, are composed of prakriti (matter). Without the soul our physical body is inert. Once the soul leaves at a person's death, the physical body made from matter begins to disintegrate. Metaphorically, the physical body arose from the ashes (physical matter) and will end as ashes (either by cremation or burial).

The creation, composition and the evolution of the universe according to the Vedic Hindu scriptures are discussed in detail in the Appendix. (See pages 147–151.)

WHY GOD CREATED THE UNIVERSE

According to the Vedas, God created the manifest universe from prakriti to provide a place for the souls to move closer to Him and eventually attain bliss. It is only in the context of the universe (prakriti) that a person can live and grow and learn right from wrong. Karma and the exercise of free will are only possible within the setting of the universe. Hence, prakriti is essential;

however, the soul must learn to utilize the resources of the universe wisely so that the soul moves towards God and does not get lost amid the distractions of the material world. This is the only reason that God created the universe. Suggestions that God created the universe for personal pleasure or for an audience are not only humorous but nonsensical and foolish.

ORIGINS OF THE WORD HINDU

Up until about a thousand years ago (or less), the people of India did not call themselves or their religion Hindu. They identified themselves as *Arya* or *Bhartiya* people and called their nation, now India, either *Aryavrata* or *Bharatvarsha*. They referred to their religion as *Vedic Dharma* (religion following the principles delineated in the Vedas) or as *Sanatan Dharma* (the eternal religion). The word "Hindu" does not exist in the Vedas, the Upanishads or in other so-called Hindu sacred writings.

Hindu was a name that foreign people, such as the Persians, and later Greeks, Romans and others called the inhabitants of the regions along the course of the Indus River and its tributaries (as well as the regions beyond the Indus River). This area now comprises modern India and parts of Pakistan. The Sanskrit word for the Indus is Sindhu; the word Hindu initially represented a mispronunciation, and later, a corruption of this name. As time went on, the religion of the "Hindus" was also referred to as Hindu. The word Hindu gained popularity in India when the country was under either Muslim or British rule because there was a need to distinguish adherents of the Hindu religion from Muslims and Christians.

Definition of the word ARYA

The Sanskrit word *Arya* (är′yə) means a noble or honorable person. In this case, noble refers to having high ideals, honorable conduct and an excellent character. It doesn't mean that a person belongs to the aristocracy. An Arya is a person who follows the rules of dharma and performs noble actions. He or she lives by the highest moral standards, has greater personal integrity and demonstrates compassion for all fellow humans based upon a belief that all souls are identical. The word Arya in India (Aryavrata) was never based upon the color of a person's skin, hair or eyes but as stated above was based upon the person's character.

The word *Aryan* properly refers to a person who speaks one of the Indo-European languages. It was never intended to indicate a specific race or set of racial characteristics. This term was, of course, incorrectly used by the Nazis to refer to blond, blue-eyed Caucasians of non-Jewish origin. No such racial meaning for this word exists in Sanskrit. Further, the Swastika, which the Nazis used, later to become the symbol of hatred and evil, is actually an ancient symbol used in India at holy places, temples and other places of worship. The word Swastika is derived from the Sanskrit word *swasti*, which means blessings for well-being. Some prayers from the Vedas are called *swasti-vachan*, prayers to ask for God's blessings for the well-being of devotees and mankind.

Over the past 150 years, Western historians have often stated that Aryans invaded India from Central Asia. This theory has been generally discarded in recent years. (See Feuerstein, et al., in reference section.) The people of ancient India have long called themselves *Arya* (but not Aryan) and have always thought of themselves as the original inhabitants of India living in the valleys and plains along the rivers flowing from Himalayas. The oral history of the Aryas does not indicate they invaded or migrated to India from somewhere else. Their nation called *Aryavrata* (but not India) had contact with the peoples of Central Asia, the Middle-East, Southeast Asia, China, Egypt and Southern Europe as well as other places.

Organization of the Arya Society

The society of the Aryas was divided into four separate groups (*Varanas*), and this organization, although somewhat altered, still exists in India:

Brahmins or spiritual teachers: These were the most learned, scholarly and philosophical members of the society. Priests and teachers mainly belonged to this group. Their primary goal in life was to reach God (Brahman) and to help others along the same path. The acquisition of power and money was not important to them and most lived a life of austerity. The Brahmins' worthiness was judged by their character, their commitment to living through the rules of dharma, their knowledge and their ability to inspire others to practice dharma.

Kshatriya or warriors: These people were the masters of the science and the art of war. Rulers and soldiers mainly belonged to this group. They would sacrifice their own lives to protect the lives of others in the society. Their importance was judged by their valor, skill and ability to win over their opponents in a fair contest.

Vaishya (farmers, business people, traders and artisans): These people generated wealth and food for themselves and other members of the society. While the farmers produced food, the artisans created goods and the business people promoted commerce, making life more enjoyable for themselves and others. The entire society was therefore **dependent** upon the activities of the Vaishya class. Their worthiness was judged by their material wealth that had been acquired through honest efforts.

Shudra or laborers: Those who were neither educated nor skilled performed work for the other classes. Their value was judged by their experience. Originally, there was no untouchable class; however, eventually those members of the Shudra class who performed the most unpleasant tasks, such as cleaning the latrines or cremating the dead, became designated as such.

The division of society into four classes was originally based on education, skills, personal qualities, character, temperament, inclination and actions performed. Although learned Brahmins were highly regarded and honored, all four groups were considered essential to the functioning of society, and no class was inherently more important than the other. The superior person was the one who performed the best work in a responsible and sincere manner. Originally this class structure was not heredity based, so a Brahmin's offspring could become a Shudra as well as vice versa. But later on the Brahmins and the ruling class turned the class structure into a hereditary system so they could retain power. The qualities and talents of a person became irrelevant.

To keep the lower classes ignorant and in their place, the Brahmins deliberately misquoted Vedic Hindu scriptures. They also found divine justifications for the persistent poverty of the labor class. Note that the story told at the beginning of this section describes a household servant (Shudra) being elevated to the status of a counselor or sage (Brahmin) implying that the caste system was not rigidly and hereditarily fixed during that time.

ASHRAMAS: *The Stages of Life*

The ideal life span for a person in ancient India was considered to be 100 years or longer. The desire to live at least 100 years is revealed through many of the Vedic mantras, such as this one:

> *Om tat chakshur devahitam purustat chhukram uchcharat. Pashyema shardah shatam, jivema shardah shatam, shrinuyama shardah shatam, prabravama shardah shatam, adina syama shardah shatam, bhuyashcha shardah shatat* (**Rig Veda 7:66:16 and Yajur Veda 36:24**).

Om	*tat*	*chakshur*
God	That One is the	Eye to the Universe Who sees and knows everything

devahitam	*chhukram*
the Supreme Being and Source of all good	pure, radiant and serene

uchcharat purustat	*pashyema shardah shatam*
Who is always present before us and is always illuminating us.	By God's grace may we see for one hundred years

jivema shardah shatam	*shrinuyama shardah shatam*
may we live for a	may we hear for a
hundred years	hundred years

prabravama shardah shatam
may we speak for a hundred years

adina syama shardah shatam	*bhuyashcha shardah shatat*
may we be healthy and	in this way may we live
self-reliant for a hundred years	beyond a hundred years.

A similar prayer for long life is in mantra # 2 from the 40th chapter of the Yajur Veda translated and commented upon in Section II. (See pages 80–81.)

The 100-year life span was divided into four principal stages called Ashramas:

Brahmcharya Ashrama	0 – 25 years
Grahastha Ashrama	26 – 50 years
Vanprastha Ashrama	51 – 75 years
Sanyasa Ashrama	76 – 100 years

The word ashrama (äsh′rəmə) both in India and in the West has usually come to mean a sheltered, serene retreat specifically designated for the acquisition of spiritual knowledge. In the present context it refers to the idea that each stage of life has its own time and responsibilities.

Brahmcharya Ashrama

The first 25 years of life were designated for the attainment of both spiritual and secular knowledge. Depending upon the skills and talents, the student would later become a teacher, warrior, physician, engineer, businessman, farmer or laborer. The students were instructed in Sanskrit and they were expected to learn Vedic scriptures along with various secular subjects. During this period, the individual was expected to work hard, to become an excellent student, to practice austerity, to remain celibate and to learn to cope with any type of hardship that one might encounter, all the while retaining faith and trust in God. During these years young people would often leave home to study under the guidance of a guru.

Grahastha Ashrama

The next 25 years were focused on the duties of a householder: getting married, raising a family, working and acquiring worldly goods. Married couples were expected to live by the dictates of dharma. While some would regard these years mainly as periods of responsibilities and burdens, Hindu scriptures have placed a great deal of importance on this ashrama. This was because the whole society's foundations and the success of all other ashramas ultimately depended upon the efforts expended during the Grahastha Ashrama (*Manu Smirti 6: 89–90*).

Tradition has always maintained that it would be easier to be a hermit or a wanderer with only responsibilities to oneself than to be a householder and live by the dictates of dharma where one is also responsible for his or her family and eventually the whole society.

Vanprastha Ashrama

The next 25 years, from age 51 to 75, were meant for contemplation of the deeper meaning of life. The scriptures were studied in the context of the education acquired as a student and the experience acquired as a householder. Members of this ashrama were society's elders.

Sanyasa Ashrama

During the final part of one's life, a person was expected to renounce his personal home and belongings and live totally in the service of God. The main goals were spiritual growth, attainment of God and the service of others. These were the saintly and most respected persons in the society and they were called *sanyasis*. The public regarded them as holy, and this tradition still continues today. Once a person becomes a *sanyasi*, he or she only wears saffron-colored clothes. Nowadays, while there are many genuine sanyasis, many others are fake. They may wear the garb of a sanyasi, but their conduct is not that of a holy person, but one of a charlatan.

While these were the ideal stages of life that an individual was expected to pass through, it's uncertain what percentage of persons experienced all of them. Further, some holy men might move directly from Brahmcharya Ashrama to Sanyasa Ashrama without passing through the intervening stages.

THE HINDU SCRIPTURES

All Hindu scriptures (most of them should be properly referred to as scriptures of Aryas) are written in Sanskrit and are divided into two main groups, *Shruti* and *Smriti*.

SHRUTI

The word *Shruti* means revealed by God. The only Hindu scriptures that are regarded as Shruti are the Vedas and, at times, such related texts as the Upanishads, Brahmans and Aranyakas.

VEDA (vādə pronounced Vade like jade)

The word Veda refers to the knowledge of God and the Soul obtained by acquiring wisdom. As stated previously, the Vedas comprise a collection of about 20,000 mantras or hymns in Sanskrit.[1] Hindus believe that the knowledge contained in the Vedas was revealed directly by God to *rishis* (holy men or seers who were accomplished yogis) while in the state of *samadhi* (the highest state of yoga where the knowledge of God is directly revealed to the Soul). All Hindus, no matter how they practice the Hindu religion acknowledge the Vedas as the root source of their beliefs and the final authority on sacred matters.

Several thousand years ago, the Vedas were organized into four major branches (or *Samhitas)*: **Rig** (knowledge), **Saam** (devotion), **Yajur** (action) and **Atharva** (science). The **Rig Veda** is the oldest

---

[1] The actual count of Ved mantras is 20,349. Several prominent mantras are in more than one Veda.

literary text of any kind to be found in any of the Indo–European languages. The main message of the Vedas is how to reach God and attain peace and bliss while living in accordance with the dictates of dharma. The Vedas deal with both the spiritual, as well as secular aspects of knowledge, and include such topics as God, His attributes, the attributes of the soul, the relationships of human beings to one another and to the community, society and other living things. Knowledge of physical nature and the universe is also discussed.

The messages of the Vedic mantras are universal; they are not directed to a select population. The Vedas do not contain any history of a group of people and do not belong to the Hindus alone. They belong to all mankind. Many Western and some Indian scholars have stated that the Vedas incorporate historical references to Aryas and cite names of various geographic places of ancient India. But generally Hindus believe that the Vedas do not contain any historical references. Any similarities between the words found in the Vedas and later historical names of ancient India are coincidental. It could have been, too, that people later adopted the same names for other reasons.

The main emphasis in the Vedas is to meditate on the message and incorporate it in one's life rather than memorize and repeat the words of the mantra. Some Vedic mantras specifically emphasize this point. (Rig Veda 1: 164: 39 and Atharva Veda 9: 10: 18.) Truth is obtained through one's own personal effort and experience and cannot be gained by the mere reading, hearing or reciting the words of the Vedas or other scriptures.

It is important to note that all prayers in the Vedas are addressed to the One God and not to other deities. Max Muller, one of the most prominent European translators of the Vedas in the 19th century, stated that the Vedic prayers were addressed to multiple gods, such as the Sun god, the Fire god, the War god, the Rain god and the god of Thunder. As has already been pointed out on pages 23–27, the Vedas clearly state, "God is One but wise men call Him by different names." Mistranslations regarding the message of the Vedas, such as those of Max Muller and others, have done great disservice to Hindu religion. Western cultures also mistakenly believe that Hindu religion promotes polytheism. This error has been corrected only to some extent in recent years.

The Sanskrit used in the Vedas is rich and compact; the same words may have multiple meanings and connotations. Also, a considerable amount of symbolism has been use in an attempt to clarify the deeper meaning of the scriptures. It is therefore important when translating the mantras to understand the proper context of each word. If a truly literal translation is used, the outcome may be significantly different from the original meaning and intent. The One God has been described in a wide variety of ways in the Vedas. With the intention of stating that God is omnipresent and all–seeing, God has been described as having an infinite number of eyes (Rig Veda 10: 90: 1). Since God is formless and bodiless, it is obvious that this is merely a metaphor, not meant to be literal. One mantra describes the responsibilities of the individual to society by saying that a person should work and earn as though he had a hundred hands and then should share the earning with others as with a thousand hands (Atharva Veda 3: 24: 5). The idea is that one should earn as much as possible through hard, honest work, and then share it with others in a generous fashion.

The Sanskrit grammar of the Vedas is very strict and traditional, and even the smallest change could affect the basic meaning of the whole mantra. Most scholars believe that the Vedas have been essentially unaltered since their origin, and thus, represent the original received texts. They are unlike other Hindu scriptures where additions and substitutions have been incorporated. The Vedic mantras were passed on by oral tradition from generation to generation, from guru to pupil and from parent to child. There are still students in India who have memorized one or more of the Vedas.

The Vedic mantras contain not only very elementary but also very advanced ideas about God, indicating that God must be accessible to all no matter where a person is in his stage of spiritual development. The greater the depth one goes into understanding the message of a mantra, the more benefit one achieves.

BRAHMANAS AND ARANYAKAS

The Brahmanas (brähmən) and the Aranyakas (ärun'yəkə) are ancient treatises that expand upon the message of the Vedas and are substantially devoted to the significance and proper conduct of Vedic prayer, including its use in rites and ceremonies. They emphasize that the full benefit of the prayer may only be obtained when it is performed with a full knowledge of its meaning. They further explain that the incorporation of the meaning of a prayer into one's daily life is more important than the other details of religious practice. Many Hindus, like practitioners of other religions worldwide, are often more concerned with correctly performing the ritual than weaving the message into the fabric of their life.

UPANISHADS

The Upanishads (ōōpun'ishud') are books of wisdom that are devoted to acquisition of spiritual knowledge and wisdom. They contain philosophical commentaries on the Vedas and emphasize the real goal of human life, the attainment of God and bliss. The word Upanishad comes from the Sanskrit roots *upa* (near) and *nishad* (sitting down). These commentaries were learned by pupils sitting near a guru as he explained the intricate meaning of the text. The other meaning of the word Upanishad refers to the knowledge that helps to destroy ignorance and takes one nearer to God. By some accounts there are as many as 108 Upanishads, although only 11 are considered to be authentic (*Isha, Ken, Kath, Prashan, Mundak, Mandookya, Aitreya, Taitreya, Chhandokya, Brahadranyaka* and *Shvetashvera*). The *Ishopanishad* is essentially the same as the last chapter of the Yajur Veda except for a minor modification of one mantra and is discussed in Section II.

SMRITI

The word *Smriti* refers to scriptures recorded by man. They are much later in origin than the *Shruti*. They are divided into four main groups: Manusmriti, Itihasa (History), Darshanas and Puranas.

MANUSMRITI

Manu is believed to be the first lawgiver in India, and his commentaries in verse form make up the *Manusmriti*. It contains the code for living for individuals, families and the society in general and provides information on rights and responsibilities. It promotes the exercise of free will but tempered with self–control in conformity to the rules of dharma. Its aim is also to attain God and moksha. It includes discussions about the organization of society and the caste system, education, marriage, domestic life, ashramas, responsibilities of the rulers, laws of the state, the punishment system for offenders and many other items related to daily life. These teachings still form a significant basis for the governing of Hindu society including its laws and traditions.

ITIHASA

The word itihasa means history and specifically refers to the records and genealogy of ancient Aryavrata (Bharatvarsha or India). The two main epics here are the Ramayana and the Mahabharata. These were initially recorded in verse form similar to the Iliad and Odyssey. Both record the innate strengths and frailties of different human beings. They reveal how dharma is practiced in a variety of situations and how goodness and truth eventually triumph over evil. They serve to give the reader confidence that he or she can also pursue the right path even when confronted with obstacles and difficulties.

Ramayana is the story of King Rama (Rä'mə pronounced Raam) and his ordeals in conquering evil kings (called *Rakshasa*: see page 29) with reference to King Ravana. It records how Rama always practiced dharma despite the many calamities that befell him. Rama in the Hindu religion is revered as the ideal person, husband and king. Hindus regard *Ram Rajya*, which is the rule of king Rama, to be the ideal rule (government) on the earth. Many Hindus believe Rama to be an incarnation of God (Vishnu), living on earth as a mortal but blessed with extraordinary gifts because of his divine nature. As such Rama is worshipped all over India and there are innumerable temples in his honor.

Mahabharata (pronounced məhäb̤här′utə) is the story of the struggle of the five righteous Pandava brothers against the more powerful, 100 evil Kuru brothers. Krishna (pronounced Kris̤hnə), also believed by many to be an incarnation of God (Vishnu), was a cousin of the Pandav brothers and aided them in conquering the Kuru brothers in the "Great War of Bharat (India)" called the *Mahabharata*. The *Mahabharata* is the longest epic poem known to man and contains, in its present form, more than 100,000 verses, although it is believed to have been much shorter (10,000–15,000 verses) when first recorded by the sage Vyasa. It contains numerous spiritual and philosophical discourses. The most famous of these are the *Bhagavad Gita*, Vidur Neeti and the Dialogues of Yudhishtra and Yaksha on dharma. The Gita is a discussion between Krishna and Arjuna (the most skillful warrior amongst the Pandava brothers) about the nature of God, the soul, yoga and the attainment of God that took place on the battlefield. It is the most famous of the Indian scriptures in the West and has often been called the Hindu Bible. Its message is similar to that of the Vedas and the Upanishads. Krishna is also worshipped as God incarnate throughout India.

Western historians have usually described the Ramayana and the Mahabharata as either legends or myths. Hindus, on the other hand, believe them to be the true record of their history, onto which myths and legends have been grafted, often including supernatural forces assisting and protecting righteous persons. This is similar to what occurred in the Iliad, the Odyssey and the Bible. Hindus assign the date of the war described in the Mahabharata as being about 5,000 years ago whereas some

Western historians consider 2,900 to 3,200 years ago as more correct (Schwartsberg, et al.). Both the Vedas and the Upanishads are considerably older than the *Mahabharata*.

To the common people in India, a belief in the *Ramayana* and the *Mahabharata* are central to the meaning of Hinduism. The Vedas are certainly acknowledged as the basis of their beliefs, but in the stories of the *Ramayana* and the *Mahabharata* are people with whom they can identify. The stories provide inspiration to help them follow the path of virtue over evil. They also help to preserve their identity and continuity with their ancient culture.

DARSHANAS

Darshanas (dur'shunə) are philosophical treatises written later than the Vedas and Upanishads that systematically reorganize their messages. The word Darshana means vision, knowledge or an experience of the Real. The Darshanas also assist in understanding God, soul and physical matter and the process of finding God and bliss. There are six Darshanas. The focus of each is different. The Yoga and Vedanta Darshanas describe the nature of God, whereas the other Darshanas center on knowledge of the soul, physical matter or other subjects. Each of the Darshanas complements the others, and they are not contradictory as it has sometimes been said in the West. They are often paired into three groups: Nyaya and Vaisheshik; Sankhya and Yoga; and Mimamsa and Vedanta. They are described in the format of aphorisms and vary in numbers from 194 aphorisms in Yoga Darshana to 2,731 in Poorva Mimamsa Darshana.

Nyaya (logic or analysis) was composed by Gautam Rishi. It describes a system of logic and proof for both secular and metaphysical use. On the secular level, it emphasizes the relationship between cause and effect, as well as the proofs required to reach a conclusion. On a spiritual level, it discusses how to overcome the ignorance of confusing the identity of the soul with that of our physical body and the need for so doing in order to attain liberation (moksha).

Vaisheshik (composition and characteristics of matter) was composed by Kannad Rishi. It discusses the basic unit of matter as being atomic and states that each element has special characteristics. It describes prakriti (matter) to be eternal but not self–activated. Prakriti needs God to activate it to become the manifest universe. It explains that soul is different from matter and that understanding this difference is essential for spiritual progress. This Darshana also discusses the concepts of dharma. (See page 10.)

Sankhya (sängkhyə) (the characteristics of God, soul and prakriti) was composed by Kapil Rishi. This Darshana reveals the methods for overcoming suffering in life and finding bliss. It describes that only by correct knowledge and learning can one discriminate between *Purusha* (God), *purusha* (soul, self) and *prakriti* (material things) in a rational manner and overcome suffering. As has already been stated, God is sat-chit-anand, soul sat-chit and prakriti sat (see page 23). *Prakriti* innately does not have any conscious energy, whereas God (*Purusha*) is the Supreme Consciousness, and it is God who activates *prakriti* to make the universe and its various components manifest. *Prakriti* (material things) can be either good or bad depending on how they are used. Followers of Shankaracharya (see page 33) often identify prakriti as *maya* (illusion). In the Vedas, only the attachment to *prakriti* is considered an illusion in the search for bliss, but *prakriti* (physical matter) is otherwise always real because it is composed of tatwas, material components (see Appendix pages 147–151). When the soul identifies with and directs its attachment to *prakriti* (material things) it will find misery in the long run. It is only when the soul identifies with and seeks its attachment to God (*Purusha*, the Supreme Consciousness) that it will eventually find bliss.

This Darshana also discusses the *gunas* (innate qualities) of objects of *prakriti*, as well as the gunas of the thought processes and character of people. The three *gunas* are as follows:

Satwa: Virtue, calm, tranquility, peaceful activity, purity
Rajas: Passion, restlessness, aggressive activity, desire
Tamas: Dullness, inertia, laziness, ignorance

Every item in *prakriti* has one or more gunas with one predominating over the others. Similarly among people, every person has one or more *gunas* in his or her personal character often with one predominating over the others. A person must strive toward discarding *Tamas gunas* and then *Rajas gunas* and make the effort toward acquiring only *Satwa gunas* in life by incorporating them into daily living through thoughts, words and actions. Only when *Satwa guna* becomes the predominant guna in one's life can one reach God. This book also discusses the nature of the mind, the intellect, or *chit*, and ego among other topics. These are reviewed in greater detail under Yoga (see pages 117–125 and in Appendix (see pages 147–151).

Yoga (yōgə) (meditation) was composed by Patanjali Rishi. This is the main text on yoga in India and the only one that is considered to offer authentic yoga practices. This will be discussed in considerable detail in Section III (pages 107–144).

Poorva Mimamsa (Inquiry) was composed by Jaimini Rishi. This text logically explains that nothing in the universe happens without effort by God or the soul and that the knowledge described in the Vedas was revealed by God. The truths of the Vedas are eternal because they represent the word of God, and all other (Hindu) scriptures, including the Upanishads, are subject to the primary authority of the Vedas. The text describes how the Vedas can help one distinguish right from wrong action. Lastly, it establishes that the person who adopts the message of the Vedas in his or her life and lives according to the rules of dharma will ultimately find moksha (liberation of soul).

Vedanta (End of the Vedas) was composed by Vyas Rishi. The other name for the Vedanta Darshana is *Brahma Sutra*. The name Vedanta literally implies that it includes a summary of all the major points of the Vedas. This book contains four chapters.

The first chapter describes the attributes of Brahman (God) and God's relation to the soul and to the universe. God is described as the Creator who molded the universe from matter and without Him it could not have been created. It further discusses the validity of this knowledge in accordance with the Vedas and the Upanishads. The second chapter considers the objections that have been raised about the material presented in chapter one and how and why such objections are fallacious. The third chapter covers the main paths for attaining God and finding bliss. The final chapter describes the attributes of bliss and enumerates the rewards one obtains from making the effort to reach God and find moksha. The larger the effort and the deeper the experience, the greater the rewards.

PURANAS (po͝orän'ə)

The Puranas record the common folklore, legends and myths of India based on the lives of various incarnations of God, as well as ancient Hindu kings and saints. They are more recent in origin than the other texts. While Puranas contain many spiritual truths and wonderful prayers similar to those previously recorded in the Vedas and Upanishads, they also contain many distortions of the original messages of the Vedas because many of the metaphors used in the Vedas and Upanishads were translated literally and described as facts. A great many gods and goddesses were invented and introduced as objects of worship.

There are 18 major Puranas and several lesser Puranas. The priestly class often promoted the Puranas over the Vedas (many priests still do the same), thus introducing error in the practice of the Vedic Hindu religion. Idol worship often replaced prayer to God, the caste system was made hereditary and passive acceptance of one's fate was taught instead of right action. The priests often promoted expensive rituals that required substantial donations to themselves and used the Puranas as the authority. They would often frighten the petitioner by explaining to him that if he deviated even in the minutest detail from the ritual a great calamity would befall him and his family. Many current rituals and practices of the Hindu religion are based on the Puranas and not on Vedic beliefs. Although many Hindus might disagree, it is possible to state that the Puranas have represented a major obstacle to understanding the essence of the Vedic Hindu religion.

OTHER HINDU AND RELATED SCRIPTURES

There are many other Hindu scriptures, such as the Tantras, which are far removed from the Vedas. They have not been included here because they do not fall within the scope of this book.

Buddhism and Jainism both arose in India as reform movements against the Puranic and Tantric practices of the Hindu religion. Both religions, while incorporating several aspects of the Vedic message have strayed far from the Vedas and will not be discussed.

Over the past 2,400 years, there have been many other Vedic scholars, Hindu teachers and holy men, such as Shankara, Bhaskara, Ramanuja, Madhwa, Ramanand, Kabir, Tulsidas, Guru Nanak and more, who have promoted some of the ideas contained in the Vedas but also deviated from Vedic teachings to a variable degree. Their teachings are also beyond the discussion here.

PROPER DEFINITION OF THE WORDS
GURU AND MANTRA

In the West, the words guru and mantra have taken on popular meanings and have been used to describe many different things. The true meaning of these words is quite different from their common usage in the United States.

GURU

In the Vedic Hindu religion, a guru (gŏoroŏo) is a spiritual teacher who has mastered spiritual knowledge and has demonstrated it in the conduct of his life. His function is to help students attain such knowledge and incorporate it into their lives as well. A guru removes the darkness of ignorance from his pupils.

A true guru promotes God's message and not himself. He is expected to live a simple life of integrity that is above reproach. He is also expected to have mastered control over his senses and desires regarding material things and indulgences, such as sex and food. When gurus receive money from various sources they are expected to use what is necessary for their own sustenance and share the remainder with the rest of mankind rather than indulge in personal luxuries.

True gurus continuously work to improve their own lives by furthering their quest for spiritual knowledge with the aim of obtaining peace and bliss and sharing it with their pupils. The focus of the true guru's aspiration is God and not worldly fame, riches and power. They live by what they preach. Rather than enslaving their followers or pupils, true gurus set them free to follow God's message and seek truth for themselves. Rather than seeking fame, true gurus are offered fame and praise by their followers and the public at large.

It is obvious though that many self-styled "gurus" are frauds. They use their charisma to fool those gullible enough to follow them. Their focus is on becoming wealthy, enjoying personal luxuries and exercising power, especially by exploiting their followers. Many such "gurus" have learned to recite a few universal messages, say a few Sanskrit words and may claim to be special messengers of God. They expect their followers to live by stringent rules that they do not apply to themselves and usually demand total obedience, reverence and often worship. Such "gurus" are really cult leaders and may lead their followers astray and even further away from God. It is surprising how many so-called "educated" people will follow such charlatans.

Finding a true guru is not always easy. It requires a lot of effort and only when one encounters a person with the desired qualities should one accept him as a spiritual teacher. A good guru may also test his pupils to find out if the pupil is worthy. One can think of the master Yoda from the movie "Star Wars" as an example of a true guru.

The guru of all gurus is, of course, God. If you cannot find a satisfactory human guru, the practice of meditation, the reading of the scriptures and incorporating their message into your life will make God your permanent guru.

MANTRA

Mantra (munt′rə pronounced "muntr") is a Sanskrit word that refers to those words of a prayer or hymn, which when incorporated into the person's life or when meditated upon, will help a person to progress toward the attainment of God. *The word mantra is only used for hymns (verses) of the Vedas.* The Vedas, as previously noted, are considered to have been revealed by God to rishis (seers, wise men), and that is why mantras are regarded as sacred. The hymns of other Hindu scriptures, such as the Upanishads, the Gita or the Brahmans, are generally called other names like *Kandika, Valli, Padya* and *Shloka* but not mantra.

A mantra is not a secret incantation or a formula to win special favors, achieve success, influence people, or win elections or the lottery as the many people in the West have often thought. Some of the misuse of the word mantra probably came from the fraudulent gurus who promised solutions to all of life's problems when one chanted a secret Sanskrit phrase.

The message or prayer of a true mantra is usually *adhyatmic* (spiritual) pertaining to God, the soul or living a spiritual life. But it may also be *adhibhoutic* (inter-personal), pertaining to relationships between human beings, society, community or nations of the world, or it may be *adhidevic*, referring to the physical forces of nature. A hymn may have a spiritual, inter-personal or secular message, or two or all three messages with one predominating over the others. The mantras are not sacred prayers to one of the multiple deities. All Vedic mantras sing the glory of only One Deity, God, who in the Vedas has been given many names, but is nevertheless only One God.

Vedic mantras are usually chanted or recited as a hymn, although some of them may be sung using special rules. Normally, they are chanted or recited as daily prayers. Mantras are also chanted during *Yajna* (also spelled *yagya*), a pledge ceremony taking place before the holy fire. A few people perform yajna by themselves everyday, while the majority of Hindus have yajna performed for them by a priest on special occasions, such as a wedding, birth of a child or death of a family member. Chanting or reciting mantras is a reminder and a pledge to live by the Vedic messages.

Yajna is not in any sense the worship of a sacred fire. The symbolic physical fire in yajna represents the inner spiritual flame one must ignite to enlighten the soul and follow God. It also signifies the pledge to follow the rules of dharma. If the symbolic fire does not kindle an inner spiritual flame and the person does not improve his or her character and way of living, then yajna becomes only a ritual and of little value. The incense and herbs burned during the ceremony may purify the nearby environment but not much more.

Likewise, Chanting mantras over and over, a hundred or a thousand or even a million times is of limited use unless the person adopts the message of the mantra in his daily life. A mantra should serve as a constant reminder of the right path to follow.

Some true gurus will advise a pupil to use a special mantra based upon an observation of the pupils abilities or other personal qualities. Such a special mantra is also expected to be a reminder to progress spiritually in life. It is not a secret incantation.

Because most Hindus have no knowledge or a very limited knowledge of Sanskrit, they often may not know the meaning of the mantra they have been given and will recite it as a mere ritual prayer that results in or yields little value to them. It is therefore important to understand the meaning of the mantra before chanting or reciting it and to internalize its message to obtain any true benefit.

PRAYER AND WORSHIP OF GOD

Worship of God in Vedic Hindu scriptures is divided into three interconnected components: *Stuti, Prarthana* and *Upasana.*

Stuti: Stuti is usually translated in English as praise of God or singing about God's glory. It's a reminder that God alone is Almighty and none else. Stuti, at a deeper level, implies intense love and awareness of the qualities of God as well as progressive incorporation of them in one's own personal life.

Prarthana: Prarthana means prayer to God. After making one's best effort, it is asking God, The Universal Benefactor, for His blessings for being able to fulfill the request. Prayer is asking for God's inspiration and help so that we may gain wisdom, strength and determination to live a virtuous life, learn humility and to help fellow human beings (see details below under why should one pray).

Upasana: Upasana literally means getting close to God. Upasana implies meditation and through the practice of yoga, realization of the Supreme Being (see Yoga: Section III for details).

Traditionally, stuti, prarthana and upasana are performed two times a day, at dawn as well as dusk. If dusk is not a suitable time, then the bedtime hour is acceptable. It is recommended that one should try to spend at least half an hour at each session in a quiet area of the house and avoid all distractions. If a person thinks that he (or she) cannot spare half an hour from daily affairs, this individual needs to review his priorities to determine why it is not possible. If he determines that certain personal, financial or other responsibilities are too great so that he cannot genuinely spare the half-hour of time, then any amount of time is worthwhile. The personal spiritual rewards gained from the limited time spent in earnest prayer will usually far outweigh those obtained from time devoted to secular affairs.

Prayer is discussed in more detail in the following four sections, "Why Should One Pray?", "To Whom Should One Pray",

"What Should Be Said in Prayer" and "The Role of Ritual and Ceremony in Prayer".

WHY SHOULD ONE PRAY?

In the Vedic Hindu religion it is only to God, the Supreme Being, that one should pray. The main reason for praying is not to flatter or to admire God, since God is not vain, but rather to express our thanks to God for providing all the good things of our life. In daily life it is not uncommon to thank people for the little kindnesses that they render to us. How great though are the kindnesses that God has done for us in comparison to these little things? Prayer, however, is not flattery of God; true prayer is sincere. Praying teaches us humility and reminds us that we are not all powerful like God. It also helps us acknowledge our limitations and our vanity so that we know where we need to improve. Praying reminds us that God is kind, just and loving, qualities that we need to acquire if we are to come close to God. Praying also reminds us of our moral duties (dharma) both to ourselves and to others and further shows us that we should seek God's counsel first and then that of our fellow humans, not the other way around.

According to Vedic scriptures, the aim of praying is for God's blessings and to obtain what has been summarized in the following four words: *Dharma, Artha, Kama* and *Moksha*. To accomplish these four goals, however, requires a personal effort (karma) and a commitment to follow a virtuous life.

Dharma: Dharma, which has been discussed on pages 10–22, means to follow a virtuous and moral path in life.

Artha: Artha means material wealth. Vedas and other Hindu scriptures have always encouraged one to earn as much material wealth (prosperity) as possible but always in the context of dharma, by honest and fair means (Rig Veda 10: 121: 10). Once wealth is acquired we are not to become so attached to it that it serves as a bondage or a burden in life's journey. It does not travel with us to our next life. Also, prosperity is to be shared with others. (Also see pages 31–32 and 77–80.)

Kama: Kama (kä'm) means fulfillment of desires, but again in the context of dharma. Vedic scriptures recognize that as human beings we are all at different stages of spiritual progress, and we have many desires and wishes that we want to fulfil as well as many shortcomings and sufferings that we want to overcome. As children we asked our parents to help us meet these needs, and as adults we seek help from friends and relatives. In the Vedic Hindu religion, God is considered not only the Ultimate Father but also our Ultimate Mother and Friend. It is therefore quite natural to pray to God, the Ultimate Benefactor, for help and assistance. Kama in the West is often mistranslated as sexual desire, such as in Kamasutra; however, the correct definition is stated above.

Moksha: Attainment of moksha, which has already been explained in detail on page 5, must always remain the ultimate goal of life. The fulfillment of artha and kama should never supersede the final goal of moksha.

God answers our prayers in marvelous and sometimes unforeseen ways, sometimes by fulfilling our prayer requests, and at other times giving us the courage, strength and wisdom to deal with the situation.

Sincere prayer and meditation, when performed in quiet solitude and with faith and devotion, will help us obtain God's grace and will bring us peace, joy and bliss. Our self-confidence and self-esteem are also strengthened but not in an egotistical way. Praying helps us distinguish right from wrong and to follow the right path and seek truth without fear. Praying will often open a clear path when one is lost in a jungle of choices and distractions. A spiritually advanced person only prays for God's grace and the well-being of mankind. He or she does not pray for specific personal gains or for material wealth because God will give all of us what we need. Therefore, such a person prays only to follow God's will and to do God's work with a prayer such as, "Dear God, Thy will be done" or "Thy grace be upon everyone".

There are a few things one should remember about prayer:

- One must never pray for impossible things (such as asking that the sun rise in the West). It is wrong to test God.

- One must never pray for the harm or the destruction of others.

- One should never pray for help without first having made one's best effort. Prayer is not a substitute for action (karma). God helps those who help themselves.

- Prayer does not mean chanting God's name over and over but requires one to make an improvement in his character and conduct of life. Prayer is also a time for self-reflection and to think about whether or not one has become more virtuous by discarding personal vices. Without an attempt to change one's life, prayer is not only useless but also hypocritical.

- One must pray on one's own behalf instead of asking the priest to do so. The role of priest is that of teacher, guide and confidante to help a person understand the spiritual aspects of life and to teach someone how to pray and meditate. Accepting donations or listening to confessions may be the duties of a priest, but they do not substitute for one's own active participation in prayer. It is sometimes the custom in India for priests to recommend special rituals for fulfillment of various desires or perhaps for the atonement of bad deeds (sins). Only a false priest would demand donations and state that he alone can perform the ritual properly. This is a deception practiced in the name of God by one of those false priests who are more interested in fleecing the gullible public for personal gain, instead of being a true teacher. A genuine priest will always live a model and virtuous life and should always be given both respect and admiration.

- While one should not ask others to pray on one's behalf, it is perfectly appropriate to pray for the well-being of others. It is a generous and unselfish gesture and may include praying for wisdom for your enemy so that the two of you may reconcile your differences.

In summary, one prays not only for one's personal spiritual, mental and physical welfare but also for that of others, extending one's requests to all mankind and nature as well. Most of the prayers in the Vedas are for "**us**" rather than for "**me**," with great deal of emphasis on being generous and giving to others because this allows one to receive God's blessings (see page 31–32 for details on being generous).

TO WHOM SHOULD ONE PRAY ?

Is one to pray to God alone or is he or she to use an intermediary image of God, such as an idol, icon or some other symbolic representation of God? Almighty God was never born, will never die and has neither shape nor form. Since this description of God may seem rather abstract to many people, it is not unusual that man has often created images of God that have human or human-like appearances.

In the Hindu religion, God has been represented in human form as Rama or Krishna and in Christianity as Christ. People have also created images of God in the form of various deities bestowing on them the qualities that they want God to have. Hindus have created the images usually in the form idols of "God's incarnations," holy persons, gods or physical objects (that represent some attribute of God), and it is for this reason that Hindus have often been accused of being polytheistic or idol worshipers. Many Christians, specifically many Roman Catholics, also pray before icons (idols, statues) of Christ, the Virgin Mary or various saints, a practice which Hindus do not find different from their own practice.

Some people (including many Hindus) find visible symbols of God in God's creations, such as the universe, the sun, the moon, the majestic snow-capped mountains or the vast ocean and pray before these aspects of nature.

In the Vedas the emphasis has always been on praying directly to God and to no other being (Atharva Veda 20: 85: 1). In Vedas there is no mention of idol worship or praying before other images of God, and in fact, one Veda mantra specifically states that omnipresent but formless God cannot be adequately represented by an image, such as an idol or a picture (Yajur Veda 32: 3). Praying to an image can be regarded as a way of trying to limit God, who is without limit. Any image of God that we can create will only have those qualities we can envision and represent in the image, and thus limit our conception of God who is Infinite.

The author of this book strongly believes and recommends that one should pray directly to God and not to an idol, icon or a picture. However, if it is easier or more comfortable for someone to pray to a created image of God while directing his prayer to God, this may be one way to begin praying. One should just keep in mind that he is praying to God and not to the image, whatever that image may be—man made or natural. Many Hindus who pray before the idols often acknowledge this limitation by the following prayer:

Dear God I ask your forgiveness for my following three shortcomings:

1. God, You are everywhere, but I worship You here.
2. You are without shape or form, but I worship Your image in various forms.
3. You need no praise, but I offer You my prayers and homage anyway.

It is unfortunately true that the offering of gifts, flowers or money to an idol may end up in distracting the individual from a focus on God. Priests who anoint idols sometimes exploit this aspect of faith by attributing ridiculous "magical" powers to them such as the recent "idols drinking milk" episode in India or icons shedding tears in the West. This is silliness, plain and simple.

It is a good policy to avoid worship before an idol or an icon since God desires neither money nor gifts. The only thing that God wishes from human beings is that they live virtuously, be generous and be of service to their fellow humans.

Donating money to help others with no desire for anything in return is immensely virtuous. However, the giving of ill-gotten gains to atone for bad deeds is, in fact, a bribe and is not a virtuous act.

There was a saint in India whose name was Kabir.[1] He was also a poet and lived around the year 1400 CE. In his simple but meaningful couplets he summarized the essential message about prayer while rejecting the practice of ritual then common in both the Hindu and Muslim religions. He emphasized the oneness of all human beings and said that the same God, whom he preferred to call Ram (Rama), had created all. Salvation, he said, is obtained by devotion to the Lord and by living according to moral principles, not by the use of ritual and show.

Unfortunately, his message was not popular with some of the brahmin pundits of the Hindu religion and the mullahs of the Muslim faith, but his piety has earned him love and admiration from the common people of India up to the present.

1. Nothing that I have is mine,
    It is all a gift from Thee;
   Why should I be reluctant to give to Thee,
    All that Thine be?

2. The stone idol in the temple
    Is not at all God;
   The One that dwells in every soul,
    He alone is the Lord.

3. You carve an idol of stone as God
    And worship it, my dear;
   Be sure if you depend on it,
    You will drown in mid-river.

---

[1]Kabir was born to a widowed Hindu mother who abandoned him when he was an infant. In his youth, he was raised by Muslim parents. Thereafter, he learned devotion to God from renowned Hindu saint Ramanand.

4. If worship of a stone idol could lead one to God,
   Then I will worship the mountain;
   For now I find grindstone better, it grinds the corn,
   Helps feed the world and seems more humane.

5. O Mullah, in mosque you shout loud your prayer,
   Is your Lord deaf that He cannot hear;
   Hear, for you know not His power,
   Even an insect's footfall He can clearly hear!

6. The fingers move the prayer beads,
   The tongue His name does whisper;
   But if your mind roams here and there
   That cannot be called prayer.

7. Who for mere show chants God's name
   But never in quiet solitude;
   The Lord's Name does not enlighten
   And such a heart remains dejected.

8. Do your duty that is best
   Treading the right way;
   That will lead you to God,
   So does the Lord say.[1]

---

[1]Seven of these eight couplets are reproduced (with minor modifications) from the English translation of Select Kabir Dohas (couplets) by Mr. GN Dass and are being included by permission of the publisher.

WHAT SHOULD BE SAID IN PRAYER?

One can pray to God in so many different ways using a variety of prayers. The majority of the Vedic mantras are prayers to God, and one can sing His praises with any one of them. As stated earlier, in addition to thanking God, praying requires a commitment to try to improve one's life and follow the message of the prayer. Other prayer options include some of the following:

1. **The constant repetition of the name of God, usually as Om,** with sincere devotion and the recognition that God alone is the Supreme Power of the universe, the Eternal Truth and the Source of all our blessings. When we ask His blessing we make a commitment to live rightly and follow the rules of dharma. In yoga, the silent chanting of Om in one's mind in similar fashion is used for both concentration and meditation. However, as stated earlier, chanting of name of God with a wandering mind, or without living a virtuous life is of very limited use, and at times, hypocritical.

2. *Gayatri* **mantra:** This is the first and most common mantra learned by most Hindus as they begin to take up the Vedas. This mantra is very important and is included in three of the four Vedas. It is recited both as a daily prayer as well as on special occasions. The words are: *Om bhur bhuvah swah. Tatsavitur varenyam bhargo devasya dhimahi. Dhiyo yo nah prachodyat* (Rig Veda 3: 63: 20, Yajur Veda 3: 35 and Saam Veda 6: 3:10:1). Its meaning is as follows:

Om	*bhur*	*bhuvah*	*swah*
Dear God You are,	the Giver and Sustainer of all life,	the Remover of all sorrows,	the Bestower of bliss.

Tat savitur	*varenyam*	*bhargo*
The Creator of the Universe, the One who always inspires us,	You alone are worthy of worship,	You are the Light which illuminates us, the Fire which burns away all our evil desires.

devasya	*dhimahi*	*yo*
You are the Supreme Being,	we meditate on Thee.	You who have all these qualities,

prachodyat	*nah*	*dhiyo*
please inspire,	our	intellect so that we move forward, may be able to tell right from wrong and always follow the right path.

3. *Om vishwani deva savitar duritani parasuva. Yad bhadram tanna asuva* (Rig Veda 5:82:5, Yajur Veda 30:3).

Om	*deva*	*savitar*	*parasuva*
Dear God,	Supreme Being,	Creator of the Universe, the One who inspires us,	please remove

vishwani	*duritani*	*yad*	*bhadram*
all forms of	vices and sorrows from us,	and those	qualities which are noble

tanna asuva
please give us.

4. *Om asato ma sada gamaya*
   Tamaso ma jyotir gamaya
   Mrityor ma amritam gamaya   (*Shatpath Brahman*).

Om	*ma gamaya*	*asato*	*sada*
Dear God	lead us from	untruth and the unreal to	truth and the real,

Ma gamaya	*tamso*	*jyotir*
lead us from	darkness and sin to	light and virtue,

Ma gamaya	*mrityor*	*amritam*
lead us from	death and misery to	immortality and bliss.

The prayer reinforces the commitment to truth, virtue and the goal of finding God. We believe that God will always lead us because God is the Ultimate Leader even though we recognize that the effort to progress along this path is ours alone. This prayer is then both a commitment to our goals and a request for God's blessing to give us strength and courage to accomplish it.

5. *Om shanno mitra sham varuna shanno bhavatu arryama. Shanno indra brahaspati shanno vishnu urukrama* (Rig Veda 1:90:9, Yajur Veda 36:9, Atharva Veda 16:6:6).

Om	*shanno*	*mitra*
Dear God	give us your blessings and peace for	You alone are our dearest Friend and closest Companion,

sham	*varuna*
give us your blessings and peace for	You alone are Most High and Most Noble.

shanno	*bhavatu*	*arryama*
give us your blessings and peace for	You alone are	the Judge who gives justice and rewards us according to our karma.

Shanno	*indra*	*brahaspati*
Give us your blessings and peace for You alone are	Master of all riches and King of all Kings, and	the Great One, the Source of all knowledge,

shanno	*vishnu*	*urukrama*
give us Your blessings and peace, for You alone are	Omnipresent, Preserver of the universe,	most powerful One who maintains the order in the Universe.

This mantra sings of the glory of God by describing seven of His supreme qualities. The several names of God used in this mantra are referring to the same One God. This mantra asks God for His blessings and peace so that, so endowed, we may improve our lives and move onwards in our life's journey. Peace and protection in this mantra are sought at three levels: a) personal spiritual, mental and physical well-being; b) interpersonal relations with other human beings and all living things; and c) the environment including protection from the sun, wind, water, famine, earthquake and pestilence (see page 53).

6. *Om agne vratpate vratam charishyami tat shakeyam tanme*
    radhyataam. Idmaham anritat satyam upaimi
    (Yajur Veda 1: 5).

Om	*agne*	*vratpate*	*vratam*
Dear God,	our Ultimate Leader,	Judge and Master Keeper of all vows,	as I take a solemn vow,

charishyami	*tat shakeyam*	*tanme*	*radhyaatam*
please bless me so that	I may fulfill my vow	and that my vow	may be successful.

Idmaham	*anritat*	*satyam upaimi*
with Thy blessing I now pledge	to reject all falsehood	and adhere to truth for the rest of my life.

Truth is one of the main pillars upon which the Vedic Dharma is built, declaring that the truth ultimately always prevails. This mantra reminds us of the fact that, in our daily lives, we often shortchange truth in many small (and sometimes big) ways. To overcome this tendency, this mantra is a pledge to always uphold the truth and to avoid falsehood in all aspects of our lives. "Lord, you are the judge of how well we keep our promises and pledges" reminds us that God is the Master Keeper of vows because all creation abides by His universal rules, while we alone because of our fears or laziness or other defects, may break our vows. "Dear God, give me Your blessing so that by Your Grace I may be successful in fulfilling my pledge" has special significance because God's blessings are usually asked for "us," but in the case where a pledge is made it becomes an individual matter.

It is always possible to compose one's own prayers, which may be useful personally in life, and it is always possible to have a collection of prayers to use that vary day to day and that can be used as needed.

THE ROLE OF RITUAL AND CEREMONY IN PRAYER

Although the author has been fairly critical of rituals so far, this is not to say that rituals have no useful purpose in prayer and worship. Rituals serve as powerful reminders of one's obligations to follow truth and virtue (dharma) in life and refrain from vices and distractions. They can help people develop good personal habits such as self-discipline, as well as sustained practice (*anushasnam* and *abhyasa:* see pages 115 and 127) so necessary in meditation. Moreover, children and the uninitiated are often initially attracted to the performance of the religious rites and ceremonies. Thus, rituals can be a wonderful way to introduce prayer and worship, which gradually pave the way for meditation. Children, however, must be taught that the intent of the ritual is prayer to God; the ritual is not an end to itself or a substitute for following dharma or meditation. Ultimately, one must remember that it is far more important to incorporate the message of the genuine prayer in the fabric of one's life rather than correctly perform the ritual since it is only symbolic and not the essence of prayer and worship.

Organized group religious activities and ceremonies in Hindu religion are called *Satsang.* This Sanskrit word literally means the company or gathering of truth seekers and truth followers. It is the equivalent of a congregation or a prayer service in the West. This gathering can be at a temple, some other place of worship or a person's home as long as the purpose is to promote God, truth and dharma. At some religious institutions in India, Satsang is a daily event, while at others it is a once weekly activity. Vedic Hindu religion (like many other religions) has always recognized that humans are social beings. We learn from each other and are likely to follow the habits and customs of the company we keep. It is at a Satsang where one is likely to hear an inspiring sermon, find a guru or meet a peer. In his simple, yet descriptive words, Kabir said the following about Satsang:

The company of the good and wise
 is like fragrance emanating from a perfumery,
Wisdom comes like the fragrance,
 whether one is a perfume buyer or a passerby.

Thus, the Satsang can assist in attaining spiritual advancement, but it must not become a replacement for personal prayer and meditation or following dharma.

SOME MISCONCEPTIONS OF THE HINDU RELIGION

As previously noted, there has been considerable misrepresentation of the Hindu religion in the West. It has often been presented as a religion of multiple gods where people worship both animate and inanimate objects, and where one can obtain salvation by chanting "secret mantras." Many are also under the false impression that one's eventual fate is sealed at birth, which promotes total acceptance and passivity, and that Hindus are always reflecting on the past, with little concern for the present or the future. A superficial look of the Hindu religion, especially as many Hindus practice it, might support such ideas. Nevertheless, at its core, the Vedic Hindu religion is quite different from these notions.

Also, people practicing the Hindu religion do not significantly differ from the way other people in the West practice their religion. For example, while Christians may believe that one should love his neighbor and turn the other cheek as preached and practiced by Christ, people usually don't do this. Many Christians pray before statues or icons of Christ or the Virgin and other saints and often light candles and bring offerings. This is not any different from the average Hindu praying before images of various Hindu deities.

It is certainly possible to find shortcomings and specific practices to criticize in any organized religion, but this is not the issue. It is the strengths of the religion that should be focused on rather than the weaknesses. Criticism of Hinduism needs to be balanced, as does that of any other organized religion.

In the West, especially in the general press, most of the emphasis has been about the superficial rituals and practices of the Hindu religion such as worship of various gods and goddesses or the fraud gurus. However, it is almost never mentioned that the Vedic Hindu religion at its core is a monotheistic religion with One and only One God and that it is the oldest continuous religion where same prayers are still sung to the same One God.

The West has also overlooked the strengths that helped the Hindu religion persevere despite 700–800 years of Muslim rule followed by 200 years of the Christian British Raj. Christianity and Islam were very effective in uprooting the older religions of Rome, Greece, the Middle East, Europe, Africa and the Americas. Like the Jews, the Hindus preserved their ancient religion despite persecution and foreign rule and kept reading the ancient scriptures and chanting the ancient prayers contained in the Vedas, the Upanishads and the Gita as they had been doing for thousands of years. Indeed, it was their religious beliefs that gave them the strength to deal with the alien forces of oppression. Even in the face of corrupt Hindu practices by the majority of members in the priestly class, the essential core of the religion remained intact and continued to be passed down from one generation to another. It was fortunate indeed that at those difficult times a few saintly Hindu individuals continued to spread the true message of the Vedas by word and deed.

As Hindus do not think that the One God of the Christians is any different from the One God called Om or Brahman; they don't consider a belief in Jesus to be any different from their belief in Rama or Krishna. Certainly many Hindus believe that God can be incarnate as a human, although the Vedic Hindu religion does not support this concept. As Hindus watch Christian religious processions featuring icons of saints or the Virgin Mary, they often regard it to be similar to processions in India where idols or other representations of Kali or Ganesh are displayed.

With so many similarities, it has been difficult for Hindus to understand why Christian missionaries claim Christianity as the only true religion. Hindus wonder what fundamental truths Christianity offers that Hindu religion does not. They see no need to replace their belief in God's incarnation as Rama or Krishna with Jesus or replace Hindu gods with Christian saints. Similarly, Hindus do not view Allah as different from Om and Mohammed as different from other messengers of God born in India.

Christ is as essential to the Christian faith as Mohammed is to Islam. If either Christ or Mohammed were excluded, the respective religions would be hardly recognizable. If, on the other hand, Rama, Krishna or other deities were absent from the Vedic Hindu faith, the religion would not have changed very significantly since God alone is perceived as the central figure.

Buddha was an Arya (Hindu) prince named Gautama (also Siddhartha) who renounced his grooming for the throne to become an ascetic and seek enlightenment. Following his enlightenment he was called Buddha, which means *the awakened one*. He emphasized that good conduct in life was far more important than rituals, blind faith or rote knowledge of scriptures. Most of Buddha's teachings are based on the Vedas and Upanishads, and he never negated God in any of his teachings. Therefore, it is hard to believe that Buddha himself did not believe in God. His teachings (which later became the basis of Buddhism) primarily arose as a reform movement against the then prevailing Puranic (see page 50) practices of Hindu religion. In parts of India, for a few centuries after Buddha's death, Buddhism was the state-sponsored religion. From India, Buddhism spread to and took root in Sri Lanka, South East Asia (Burma, Thailand, Cambodia, Vietnam and Indonesia), Central Asia, China, Japan and Korea.

Buddhism, however, never gained a strong hold in India because Buddha's followers rejected the existence of God and the authority of the Vedas and worshipped Buddha like a deity. On the other hand, many Hindus, while willing to incorporate Buddha as one more incarnation of God (Vishnu), were unwilling to replace their belief in One God called Om or Brahman with Buddhism.

Although much has been said of Hindu passivity, the religion is really very action oriented. Dharma is based upon action rather than faith alone. Similarly, the concept of karma clearly states that man determines his own fate; God only administers it. According to this concept, one should accept what one cannot change *only* after having tried to make things better.

The criticism that Hindus always look to the past is also shortsighted. A Hindu must look to the present and the future since that is where all new karma is. The reason many Hindus look to the past is for the guidance and inspiration that can be found there, and this is also true for many other religions as well.

THE WAYS TO REACH GOD: DIFFERENT RELIGIOUS VIEWS

Many thoughtful people have said that all religions are basically the same and that all paths lead eventually to God. This has been construed to mean that it does not matter which religion one belongs to or how one practices his or her faith. It is true that there are certain basic truths common to all major religions and that each has its strengths and weaknesses. One should learn and incorporate into his/her life the most positive aspects from all faiths. But the idea that all religions are basically the same and that all paths lead to God, is not quite accurate. Consider the pictorial representation on the following page:

In going from point **A** to point **B** in this scheme, there is only one path that is the shortest, and that is path # 1, which is a straight line. Paths # 2, # 3, # 4 and # 5 are longer and more circuitous than path # 1, but they do eventually reach point B. Paths # 6, # 7 and # 8, however, would actually lead someone at point A in the opposite direction from point B. This can be compared to many religious paths as well; some are direct while

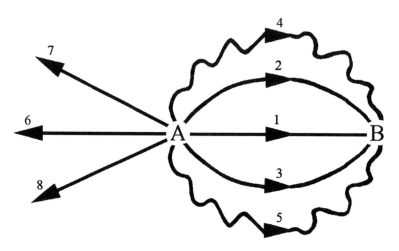

others are circuitous. And some so-called religious paths might actually move away from God, towards misery and unhappiness.

There are many religious leaders that appear to be holy and charismatic but actually are spiritual frauds or religious charlatans, preaching easy and painless solutions that gullible people may find attractive. It is important to use caution in spiritual decisions as it is in all other decisions in this life. In this regard, one might act like the honeybee that carefully selects the blossom from which to get its nectar, rather than behave like a housefly that would just as well alight upon garbage as food.

When someone searching for spiritual enlightenment encounters a new and exciting religious path it behooves him to carefully examine just exactly what is being offered. He should then make a sound decision based on reason, rather "spiritual rapture." A spiritual path that offers the most positive reward even though it may require greater personal effort to succeed is the best choice. While embarking on a particular path, a wise person will follow it with faith and devotion, never losing his common sense and discrimination.

Dharma (religion) demands that we diligently pursue the truth. The definition of dharma, as stated earlier on pages 10–22, includes: Dhriti (thoughtfulness with patience and strength),

Dhee (discriminating ability) and Satya (truth). *The truth will always ultimately prevail.*

Section II

40TH CHAPTER OF YAJUR VEDA

The emphasis in Yajur Veda is on proper deeds (karma), how to live and work in this world to reach God and find bliss. Yajur Veda has 40 chapters and 1,975 mantras. The last (40th) chapter contains 17 mantras that describe the essence of Yajur Veda and, in fact, the essence of the Vedic Hindu religion. Because of the immense importance of these 17 mantras to Vedic Hindu belief, this chapter, with minor modifications, was compiled into a separate Upanishad called Ishopanishad. Ishopanishad has 18 mantras; the 17th mantra of the 40th chapter has been modified and divided into two mantras. Also, beginning with the 9th mantra, the order of the mantras is different in Ishopanishad as compared to the 40th chapter of Yajur Veda.

This section includes a word-for-word translation of each mantra from Sanskrit to English. A discussion of the meaning and the message of the mantra follows. Some mantras, such as # 4 and 5; # 6 and 7; # 9, 10 and 11; and # 12, 13 and 14 have been grouped together because their messages are complementary and it makes the discussion easier to understand.

Mantra # 1: GOD PERVADES EVERYWHERE IN THE UNIVERSE

Eesha vasyamidam sarvam yadkincha jagatyam jagat.
Tena tyaktena bhunjitha ma gridhah kasya swidhanam.

Human beings, listen!

Eesha	vasyam	idam	sarvam
God, the Master of all riches in the universe	dwells	here around you	everywhere,

yadkincha	*jagatyam jagat*
in every spot you can imagine,	in every region of this vast and changing universe.

Tena	*tyaktena*
Therefore, you should	without attachment or craving, share with others,

bhunjitha

enjoy the riches which God has given you and
which you have earned by your actions

ma gridhah	*kasya swidhanam*
do not be greedy and do not covet	those riches which belong to others.

The second half of this mantra may also be interpreted as saying that you should enjoy, without attachment, what God has given to you. And do not covet. *Kasya swidhanam* is translated as "whose wealth is it?" Remember all wealth ultimately belongs to God. When you die you will not carry it with you.

DISCUSSION OF MANTRA # 1.

If it became necessary to describe the essence of the Vedic Hindu belief, it would be found in this mantra, and, more precisely, in its first three words—*Eesha vasyamidam sarvam*—which indicate that God is present everywhere in the vast universe, that **God is omnipresent.**

When a person develops a deep inner faith that God is present throughout the universe and realizes that God is always here as his closest companion, that God protects and guides him (through the inner voice of the soul), then he will never feel alone. This creates a sense of inner security and integrity within him. A person with this belief becomes fearless in the pursuit of truth and does not sway from the correct path. Such a person always seeks God's approval rather than that of other people.

When we realize that God watches over all our actions (karma) and judges them, we become willing to try our best to do the right thing and to resist temptation and avoid error (sin). Most humans are far more afraid of being caught committing a sin than actually performing the sin, but when someone realizes that he cannot hide from God, then the only reasonable course is not to carry out any bad deed.

In India, the following parable is often told to illustrate the omnipresence of God.

There was once a powerful Indian monarch who said to his spiritual advisor, "You always talk about the power and the glory of God, but is there any power that I have that exceeds that of God?" The counselor replied, "Of course, you have one power that exceeds that of God." The monarch then said, "I do? Tell me what that power is." The advisor replied, "Sir, you can banish any one of your subjects from your kingdom. This is something that God cannot do. He cannot banish a single subject from His kingdom!" The monarch was embarrassed and said, "That will do. I get your point."

The other meaning of the word *Eesha* in this mantra is that God is the Master of the entire spiritual and the physical wealth in the universe. All wealth belongs ultimately to God. God is the Universal Benefactor. Only God can fulfill both our physical and spiritual needs. We need only ask God for His blessings and do not need to go begging from others.

The last three words of the first part of this mantra (*yadkincha jagatyam jagat*) make it clear that the word *everywhere* refers to every last place in the universe, whether or not it can be imagined. It also reminds us that God's universe is in constant motion and undergoing continuous change. We too, then, must remain active and forever try to improve ourselves. This mantra encourages us to always make the effort and to try to do those good deeds that are explained both in the remainder of this mantra and the whole of the next one.

The last part of this mantra counsels us to live, prosper and enjoy the things of this world without being attached to them. It is useless to covet earthly riches since you will not be able to take them with you when you die; only the results of your deeds (karma) will accompany you. Above all, we are told not to be greedy and desire those things that belong to others. Instead, we are to be contented with those things that we have earned through our honest labor. In the Vedas greed is considered to be one of the root causes of unhappiness and misery in life (see page 15 under *asteya*). We are also counseled to share what we have with others, to be generous and giving (see page 31), which in contrast to greed, brings peace and happiness in life. We are only stewards of those things that are given to us on earth since all things really belong solely to God. Our goal is to attain God and find bliss and not to get enmeshed in transitory worldly pleasures and riches.

> God alone is your Master
> Everything belongs to Him;
> Pray for what you need
> Let the rest remain with Him.

Mantra # 2: WORK, DUTY, LONG LIFE AND FREEDOM FROM BONDAGE

Kurvannev eha karmanni jijivishet shatam samah.
Evam tvayi nanyathetoasti na karma lipyate nare.

Human beings listen!

Kurvannev	**eha**	**karmanni**
Conscientiously and without attachment perform	here on earth	your deeds, work and duty (karma)

jijivishet	**shatam samah.**
for only then may you expect to live	a full hundred years.

Nare	**evam tvayi**	**na karma lipyate**
Human beings,	if you live by these principles	your deeds will not subject you to bondage but rather give you freedom and bliss;

nanyathetoasti.
there is no other right path for you.

DISCUSSION OF MANTRA # 2:

This mantra explains the philosophy of karma very succinctly. The first part of the Mantra makes it clear that, so long as you are alive, you will be performing deeds or actions since that is the nature of the soul. It is only when you are working hard and doing virtuous deeds that you may aspire to live to be 100 years old. (The life span in the Vedic religion has always been envisioned to be 100 years or more. Also see pages 38–41.) The next part of this mantra reminds us that there is also no escape from performing karma so long as one is alive. Therefore, it is impossible to escape the consequences of every behavior. Another way of saying this is to point out that there is no escape from the present and the reality of life. This line also indirectly counsels against laziness, since sitting around and thinking about things without doing them will not bring any significant results. The message from God according to this mantra is that one should always aim to perform virtuous deeds for the benefit of oneself and one's fellow beings. When you perform your karma (deeds) in a selfless manner and without attachment or desire for reward, then they will free you from the bondage of desire or suffering and help you come closer to God and eventual bliss. This is the only way to liberation; there is no other. This is also the essence of Karma Yoga. (See page 110.)

As stated before (see pages 4 and 28), there has been a lot of misunderstanding regarding the meaning of the word *karma*, especially in the Western world. It is frequently thought of as being synonymous with the word fate in its passive sense and the Hindu religion has been thought of as promoting the idea of passively accepting one's fate. Nothing could be farther from the truth. Karma in the Vedic texts implies action rather than predestination or fate. As humans we decide our own fate; God only administers it. The English word closest in meaning to *karma* is deeds. A human being is free to perform any karma he may choose, but once the action has been performed, only God becomes the judge to determine the results of the karma. The results of karma, which we must experience, is called *bhoga* not karma.

Master Yogi Krishna in one of the most famous stanzas (*shlokas*) in the *Gita* says, "No matter what conditions you encounter in life, your right is only to the works—not to the fruits thereof" (*Karmanyeva adhikaraste na phaleshu kadachan*—Gita 2:47).

It is certainly true that we usually choose to do things that are based on our past experiences, the results of our past karmas. For instance, a person who has always helped others is far more likely to do so again at some future time when the need arises. Someone else, who has been exploitative and selfish all his life, will be far less willing to lend a hand to someone in need. Free will, however, allows everyone the option of changing the nature of the deeds performed. They can go from bad in the past to good in the present or future or in the opposite direction, from good to bad. Situations where greed or pride rules may cause a person to fall from virtue. The corruption of a previously honest policeman by greed may serve as an example.

The three types of karmas are classified as follows:

1. *Good Karma (Sat or Shubh)*. *Sat* refers to those deeds that help an individual to become a better person and to those deeds that are for the welfare of others or some part of the universe. Several virtuous deeds have been described in the section on dharma (see pages 10–22) and include truth, honesty, integrity, kindness, patience, courage, forgiveness, generosity, discipline, introspection, physical and mental cleanliness and purity, not coveting things not one's own, controlling one's anger and harnessing one's pride. They also include perseverance, austerity, sacrifice and studying the scriptures to acquire wisdom. The highest quality *Sat* karmas are called **Nishkama Karmas** and are done in the service of God for the welfare of others or for the physical world with no desire of any reward in return.

2. *Ordinary Karma*. Karmas that are for self-maintenance, such as eating, bathing, exercising, fulfilling requirements of a job,

playing, enjoying nature, like hiking in the woods, entertainment, having fun.

3. *Bad Karma (kukarma).* These are the karmas that move us downward in our life's journey. Included are sinful deeds that harm our inner self, other beings or the physical universe. Mantra # 3 will explore this further. (See page 86.)

Good or virtuous deeds bring rewards in the form of riches, happiness and bliss, whereas bad deeds bring pain, misery and suffering. "As you sow, so shall you reap" says the Bible. The results of some karmas are immediate (putting your hand into a fire) whereas the effects of other karmas are delayed. God alone decides when the rewards for the karmas are to be given. Nevertheless, the good and bad consequences of past and present deeds must be experienced at some time or other. Our free will allows us continuing chances to improve the nature of our decisions up to the moment of death. It is then that God decides what our next life shall be.

The present state of a person's life is the result of the accumulation of past and present good and bad karmas. Any success we achieve is based on both our present effort and the results of our past karmas. This explains why people who are living virtuously may at times be suffering or failing. This is the result of previous bad deeds and explains why bad things happen to good people. If a person is currently engaged in virtuous behavior, yet suffering, he or she should not lose heart and begin to take up evil behaviors. One must always keep faith in God's judgment and fairness and not stray from the right path since all good deeds will ultimately be rewarded.

It is important to remember that current suffering is the burning away of past bad karma, and there is much hope for the future because of the reward that current virtuous behavior will bring. One must learn to accept God's judgments as they come and not complain about one's current plight. God is always just even though we, with our limited knowledge, may not understand

His ways. Blaming others for one's suffering or shortcomings shows lack of understanding since they are the result of our own past and present karma and not that of others. We always have the opportunity to modify the future by performing virtuous deeds in the present. Our fate is not etched in stone. We are always changing it with new karma. There is no auspicious time to start good karma; every moment of life is a new opportunity to improve. It is only through this kind of action-oriented behavior that one can hope for a better today and tomorrow. Passively accepting life will not bring about its improvement.

Any work (karma) performed that is not harmful either to oneself or others is worthwhile and commendable when it is done with sincerity and with one's best effort. Likewise, it is important to be happy in one's work, especially when the circumstances cannot be changed.

Karmas can be performed at three separate levels:

a. Mental   thought / intent
b. Verbal   word / expression
c. Physical   action / execution

The following example will perhaps be useful in illustrating the three levels of karma. The thought or plan to help others is karma at the mental level. Talking to those one is trying to help and encouraging them is verbal karma. Carrying out action to help them is physical karma. All three levels are essential and usually work in synchrony. There are times when the karmas may be out of harmony, such as when a person who has no desire whatsoever to help someone else merely goes through the physical motions of pretending to help. This type of action is deception, which is bad karma. A person who spends the day cheating others and then donates some of his ill-gotten gains to charity is not performing good karma. His rewards will not come from his donations to charity but acts of cheating.

In the Vedic scriptures a great deal of emphasis has been placed on the intent behind the action. The intent of karma in

Yoga is called *karmashaya* (see page 120). For example, if you attempt to rescue a person who is falling from a roof and who is hanging onto the edge by his hands, and during your rescue attempt he slips, falls and is injured, the resulting karma is good (attempting to help someone in need). The rewards of your karma are based upon the good intentions and effort, rather than from the unfortunate result.

Donating money to a charity with the primary purpose of receiving acclaim is an ordinary karma. It may result in transient renown but does not represent a good (*sat*) karma. However, if the primary intent was to help others, and the acclaim is a side product, then it turns into a *sat* karma. A dollar donated by a poor person to a charity with no expectation of return is a much better karma than the donation of a million by a rich person who does it primarily for the reward of fame or reputation.

The final goal of all karma is to reach God and find freedom and bliss. A person who wishes to rise above the bondage of past karmas has but to perform his actions in a selfless manner without attachment (*Nishkama karma*) for the honor of serving God. For such a person, even eating and sleeping are in God's service because these activities allow him to work longer and harder in an unselfish manner. This is the sum and substance of karma philosophy and Karma Yoga and the road to freedom and bliss.

Mantra # 3: BAD OR SELF-DESTRUCTIVE DEEDS LEAD TO DARKNESS

Asurya naam te loka andhena tamasa vritah.
Tanste prety abhi gacchanti ye ke chatmehano janah.

Ye ke ch	*janah*	*atmehano*
Those	persons who	harm their soul and do things against the inner voice, commit suicide or sin

tanse	*prety*	*abhi gacchanti*	*te loka*
those people	after death	go to or are born into	those regions of the universe

vritah	*andhena tamasa*	*asurya naam.*
which are covered with	severe ignorance and impenetrable darkness	and are fit only for less than human forms, devoid of sunlight.

DISCUSSION OF MANTRA # 3

This mantra explains the consequences of bad deeds or sins (bad karma). In the Hindu religion, the cardinal sins are lying (*asatya* or untruth), lust, morbid affection (blind attachment to others and material objects), greed, anger, envy and vanity. The very worst sins, however, are suicide and killing others (except in self-defense or in a morally justifiable war). Other vices include laziness, gambling and drinking or getting intoxicated. These various sins and vices can exist at the level of thought, word or deed. They are all considered to be self-destructive and a setback in life's upward progress.

We are born as human beings as the result of our past good karma. As humans we must always be grateful for our blessings because this is the only life form in which we have a free will and an opportunity to make further progress toward God, peace and bliss. Accordingly, all human life is not only precious but sacred, and one must do nothing to harm or destroy it. Harming ourselves comes from performing bad karma and acting against the dictates of our inner voice as well as dharma. Suicide is harshly condemned because it goes against the precious opportunity that God has given us for bettering ourselves. As such, suicide is a bad karma, and the person who commits suicide will have to suffer the consequences of the act.

The consequences of various self-destructive deeds are that they lead to ignorance, misery and suffering (a truly living hell) in this life. And after death, these destructive deeds lead to being born in a less than human state (such as animal or plant), where the individual is not aware of his actions and must suffer for a prolonged period before getting the chance to be born again as a human. In Vedic Hindu religion, hell as a place of fire and brimstone does not exist but being entrapped in ignorance and suffering is considered to be hell. In Hindu mythology, hell is thought to be the most wretched physical place imaginable, and in this regard, is similar to Western beliefs. The exception is that hell is not eternal, and after suffering the consequences of previous sins one can be reborn as a human being. A literal interpretation of this mantra contains the idea that, as a result of suicide, the next life will be in a much lower form covered by a darkness so deep that even the sun does not penetrate it (such as inside a deep cave or on the ocean floor). The mantra reaffirms the idea of living a virtuous life and avoiding self-destructive behavior because the latter leads to misery in this life and suffering in future lives.

Mantras # 4 & # 5: THE OMNIPRESENT GOD

Anejadekam manaso javiyo nainad deva apnuvan
purvamarshat.
Taddhavatonyanatyeti tishthattasminnapo matarishva
dadhati. (#4)

Ekam	anejad	manaso javiyo	nainad
That One, God	does not move	but is much swifter than the mind,	the senses

deva apnuvan	purvamarshat.
cannot catch up with God	because God is already there ahead of thought, for He is Omnipresent.

Tad	tishthat	atyeti	dhavato anyan
That One, God	while sitting still	outruns	the runner.

tasmin	matarishva	dadhati	apo.
It is to that One God	that the individual soul	should dedicate	all good karma.

Tadejati tannaijati tad dure tadvantike.
Tadantarasya sarvarsya tadu sarvasyasya bahyatah. (#5).

Tadejati	tannaijati	tad dure	tadvantike
God moves	and He does not move,	God is far away	and He is near,

Tadantaraysa sarvasya	tadu sarvasyasya bahyatah.
God is inside everything	and He is outside everything.

DISCUSSION OF MANTRAS # 4 & # 5.

In both of these mantras, several apparently contradictory statements have been made to point out that God is omnipresent, omniscient and omnipotent.

While in the physical world it is the speed of light that is thought to be the fastest thing possible, the mind is an even swifter traveler for it can traverse the huge distances to the moon, sun, stars and beyond in an instant. The mind is indeed very fast, but

God is even faster, for wherever the mind goes, God is already there. Thinking further about this causes one to realize that if something is everywhere at the same moment then it does not really move. God moves and He moves not.

God is inside everything. He knows all that is going on, even in the most secret recesses of our minds. God also knows everything that is happening outside of all things. So God is omniscient. All living and non-living things, planets, stars and galaxies reside in God's universe and God surrounds all of them. Omnipresent God is limitless; He is not bound by time or space. There is no power stronger than God. Omnipotent God remaining still outruns and outdoes everything else in the universe.

God also dwells in our soul. He is the nearest entity to us. Wise persons know that God is always there inside their souls. They do not have to travel to a sacred or a holy place to find Him. Some people who are not as wise think that, if God exists, He dwells at some far away place in the universe (heaven). If we choose to make God a remote entity, then God will truly feel far away from us, although He is always with us. God cannot be perceived by our senses because they are so limited in scope.

As human beings living on the earth, we cannot even appreciate that the earth at the equator turns on its axis at about 1,000 miles per hour and revolves around the sun at about 66,000 miles per hour. There are also so many things that we can't see or feel around us.

God is perceived by our soul instead of our senses. And, when we dedicate all our activities to the service of God and become selfless in our actions, we finally find God.

Mantras # 6 & # 7:
THE REALIZATION THAT GOD IS
THE UNIFYING ELEMENT IN ALL PEOPLE
REMOVES ALL DOUBT AND BRINGS BLISS

Yastu sarvani bhutani atmanyev anupashyati
Sarvabhuteshu cha atmanam tato na vichikitsati (# 6)

Yastu	*atmanyev anupashyati*	*sarvani*
Whoever	realizes that his true self is his soul, sees a similar soul in	all

bhutani	*cha*	*sarvabhuteshu*	*atmanam*
living beings	and	in all living beings	sees the Supreme Soul, which is God;

tato	*na*	*vichikitsati*
that person	does not have	any doubts and any loathing for others.

Yasmin sarvani bhutani atmaivabhud vijantah
Tatra ko mohah kah shokah ekatvam anupashyatah (# 7)

Yasmin	*vijantah*
In the state	when a person possesses deep knowledge, like a yogi, that person sees in

sarvani	*bhutani*	*atmaivabhud*
all	living beings	similar soul as one's own soul, as well as the same Supreme Soul.

Tatra	*ekatvam anupashyata*	*ko mohah*	*kah shokah*
In that state,	seeing God as the unity in everything,	the person has no attachments	and no misery or grief.

DISCUSSION OF MANTRAS # 6 & # 7

Both mantras emphasize that all souls are similar and that it is the same God who unifies all of us. When it becomes apparent that differences between people are merely superficial and have only to do with external appearances and that all souls are similar, pure and contain the same God, then all hatred and jealousy for others will pass away and love for all of God's people will emerge. This love, called divine love, is expansive in nature, rather than restrictive. In this regard, most prayers in the Vedas are for *us* or *mankind* and not *me*. The Lord's prayer in the Bible also says, "Give *us* our daily bread," rather than "Give *me* my daily bread." Each person who so prays has replaced selfish *me* with generous *us*. In a similar fashion, we do not hate the sinner but rather the sin. This is the type of brotherly love that Christ taught when he said, "Love thy neighbor." Jealousy and hatred of others because of social status, race, ethnicity, religion or nationality brings misery to everybody. It is only by realizing that we all have the **same One God** and that our souls are similar that we can ever find peace and harmony in the world. It is not until we recognize that others have the same joys and sorrows, aspirations and goals, sufferings and misery as we do that we can apply the Golden Rule: *"Do unto others as you would have them do unto you."* Or alternately stated as, *"Do not do unto others what you would not like done to you."* Treat each person as an individual, rather than a means to some end. It is unfortunate that the "Golden Rules" often used in the world are: "Do unto others before they do unto you" or "Them that have gold (power) will rule," both of which see people not as similar beings, but as objects of exploitation.

These two mantras offer the strongest possible argument against discrimination and the idea of "untouchability," which have pervaded India's history for more than a thousand years. It is sad that there is a discrepancy between what the religion dictates and how it is practiced. This problem, of course, is not unique to the Hindu religion. Until relatively recently, many white Christians and Jews practiced and justified racism. One example was evidenced by the separation of common facilities for blacks and whites in both the United States and South Africa because black people, like untouchables, were considered less than human. How can someone really believe that there is One God and that the same God exists in all persons and still not find kinship with all fellow humans?

Lastly, it should be recognized that only God is permanent and that all worldly relationships and material things are transient and do not accompany the soul after death. This realization allows us to rise above these attachments and learn to surmount grief caused by the loss of interpersonal relationships and worldly goods and develop peace and equanimity. It is true that when a person becomes enlightened to the Oneness of God in all aspects of life, seeing the glory of God everywhere, that person overcomes all doubts and fears and achieves salvation and bliss. This is also the final goal of yoga.

MANTRA # 8: THE ATTRIBUTES OF GOD

Sa paryagat shukram akayam avarnam asnaviram shudham apapviddham.
Kavirmanishi paribhu svayambhuh yathatathyatoarthan vyadadhat shashvatibhyah samabhyah.

Sa	*paryagat*	*shukram*	*akayam*
God,	is located everywhere,	is pure radiance,	is bodiless,

avarnam	*asnaviram*	*shudham*
is without any bodily vulnerability,	is devoid of any nerves or sinews,	is completely pure and holy

apapviddham	*Kavir*	*manishi*
is untouched by sin or evil.	God is Omniscient and knows the minutest details of everything,	Wisest, Seer, most knowledgeable of past, present and future

paribhu	*swayambhuh*	*shashvatibhyah*	*vyadadhat*
transcendent,	self-existent, never born nor died,	since eternity	has been distributing and providing

yathatathya	*arthan*	*samabhyah*
appropriate, based on our deeds	all provisions	for all beings.

DISCUSSION OF MANTRA # 8

This mantra re-emphasizes that there is but One God who has many attributes. Based on these attributes, as described in the Vedas and other Hindu scriptures, God has been given hundreds of names but this does not divide Him into separate gods. Here God is described as the Total Master of the Universe. Those attributes of God that are brought out in this mantra are as follows:

- God is everywhere; God is omnipresent; it is impossible to hide from God or to feel that one's actions are not seen by God

- God is Pure Radiance; God is the Ultimate Power, Force and Energy in the Universe. It is only by finding God that one can achieve enlightenment in life.

- God has no physical body; God is not flesh and blood as are humans. Further, God is neither masculine nor feminine but **simply God.** Of course, it is possible to address God as either He or She, but this does not make God either female or male. God is devoid of shape and form, so it is not possible to make an image of God in a painting, idol, icon or a statue.

- God was not born and will never die. God transcends time. God always has been and always will be. God existed before time and before eternity and will exist after the end of time and beyond eternity. (The Vedic Hindu religion disagrees with the concept of God's being incarnated as Rama, Krishna or Christ.)

- God is pure and holy, thus devoid of any evil and any sin. It is only by following God's path that one can overcome evil and find holiness in one's own life. Visiting shrines and holy places are only important in that they remind a person about God and help him to find God. Bathing in the river Ganges (Ganga) or being baptized with holy water do not alone provide salvation; salvation is only found by good deeds and devotion to God.

- God knows everything; God is omniscient. He knows the smallest details about everything that exists, seen or unseen. God the Seer has the ultimate vision and knows the past, the present and the future.

- God alone is the Ultimate Master and Final Judge in the Universe. He possesses all the riches in the universe and distributes them appropriately to all depending upon the past and present deeds.

- God is the Ultimate Benefactor and Provider. God alone nurtures and cares for the earth and the universe. God provides for the needs of all living things whether man, bird, animal or other creature. God will, therefore, always provide for our needs if we have faith and make the necessary effort.

- Therefore, it is essential that we pray only to God the Ultimate Reality and none else.

Mantras # 9, # 10 & # 11:
THE INDIVIDUAL AND SOCIETY

Andhamtamah pravishyanti ye asambhutim upasate.
Tato bhuya iva te tamo ya u sambhutyam ratah. (# 9)

Ye	*upaste*	*asambhutim*
Those persons who	pursue and worship,	individualism

pravishyanti	*andhamtamah*
enter	deep darkness

ya u	*ratah*	*sambhutyam*
and those who,	pursue or delight in	collective well-being of everyone in society,

te	*tato bhuya iv*	*tamo*
they,	enter even greater	darkness.

Anyadevahuh sambhavad anyad ahur asambhavat.
Iti shushruma dhiranam ye nastad vichachakshire. (#10)

Ahur	*sambhavad*	*anyadev*
It is said, that pursuit of	collective well-being of everyone in society,	has distinct results.

ahur	*asambhavat*	*anyad*
It is also said that,	individualism	has distinct results.

Iti	*shushruma*
This	we have heard from

dhiranam	*ye*	*vichachakshire*	*nastad*
seers, wise persons	who	have explained and expounded	these matters to us.

Sambhutim cha vinasham cha yastad vedobhayam saha.
Vinashen mrityum titarva sambhutya amritam ashnute.
(#11)

Yas	*ved*	*tad obhyam saha*	*sambhutim*
Those, who	understand and pursue	side by side	the collective well-being of everyone in society

cha cha	*vinasham*	*titarva*
as well as	individualism,	conquer

mrityum	*vinashen*
misery and death	with the pursuit of individualism, and

ashnute	*amritam*	*sambhutya*
attain	immortality and bliss	with selfless service for the well-being of everyone.

DISCUSSION OF MANTRAS # 9, # 10 & # 11

Mantras 9, 10 and 11 describe the significance of individualism, together with the promotion of the collective well-being of everyone in the society. The word *asambhuti* in these mantras (or *vinashen* in mantra # 11) means individual/individuality and the word *sambhuti* refers to human beings collected together into a society or community. The word-for-word Sanskrit-to-English translation given above for mantras 9 and 11 may appear at the outset to be confusing or conflicting. However, it will be seen that the seemingly paradoxical statements have been used as a means of clarifying the significance, as well as both the benefits and liabilities of individualism and promotion of societal well-being, depending on how these are practiced.

Mantra # 9 says that human beings who choose individuality at all cost—spend all their energy in personal enrichment or gratification, especially by exploiting others or the environment and/or use unfair means such as bribery or dishonesty—live in ignorance and will ultimately end up in misery. These are the *me* people: "What's in it for me?" "How will it affect me?" —without regard for the welfare of fellow human beings. These are narcissistic people whose goal in life is personal power and glory. This type of individuality, as considered in the explanation of mantras # 6 and # 7 (see pages 90–92), is about selfishness and envy and is not related to generosity and love. Such persons may succeed for a while, but eventually they experience a downfall because of their selfishness and arrogance.

When viewed in terms of the society as a whole, the counterpart of such selfish individuality is exploitative capitalism. Similar to exploitative individuality, exploitative capitalism in the short run may make enormous profits for those that use it, but it too, will experience a collapse later on. This type of capitalism usually exists in the less industrialized countries where the wealthy exploit the laboring classes and pay them substandard wages while amassing substantial personal wealth. Such societies and corporations eventually suffer failure because they fulfill the desires of a select few at the expense of the society as a whole. The ninth mantra also states that those individuals or societies which promote the benefits of collective well-being or conformity to societal rules, whether right or wrong, are *even worse* than those who promote individuality. Many of the collective farms and state-operated concerns of the old Soviet Union are examples of such collective well-being policies (collectivism, socialism or communism). This mantra clearly states that individuality (capitalism) is always preferable to collectivism (socialism). Without individual freedom or the possibility of personal initiative, people almost never put forth their best efforts.

The next mantra, # 10, explains that wise men who have reflected on the pursuit of individualism and promotion of societal well-being have perceived that both have distinct results that can be either harmful or beneficial depending on how they are achieved. This mantra also implies that, when one has a problem deciding between rights of the individual and the rights of society as a whole, it is best to seek the advice of a wise man or a sage.

Mantra # 11 makes the point that both individualism and promotion of collective well-being of society can be of great value for the individual and the society if both are practiced in the spirit of generosity. When one has the courage, integrity and determination to carry out a task despite the odds against its success, when one pursues the truth and virtue, irrespective of the circumstances, or when one maintains personal honesty and integrity in the face of a largely corrupt society, this is the type of individuality that is laudable. This mantra says that such individuality conquers death (unhappiness in life). Such a person finds inner happiness and joy, which will sustain him; he does not need others accolades to go on. The mantra additionally says that, in order to find bliss, one must not be content with personal gains but willing to share them for the good of all. It is only when one is able to transcend one's own personal goals for the welfare of everybody in the society and not expect anything in return that one truly finds bliss and attains God.

The messages of these three mantras may be summarized as follows:

1. Both the rights of the individual and those of the society are important and must be properly balanced. It is important to have freedom in one's personal affairs and in those things that affect one's well-being, but each individual must be subordinated to the rules of society (as long as the rules are just). In a society, individual initiative and enterprise is always preferable to policies of collectivism or socialism. It is the duty of the society to restrain the individual from being exploitative of other humans or the environment.

2. Any individual should be free to expend whatever effort he or she pleases on achieving personal progress and prosperity. On the other hand, one must never be content with one's own well being alone and must accept responsibility for the welfare of the community and the prosperity of others. Each member of a society is dependent upon other members of the society as well as nature and the environment. This is the way for an individual and a society to overcome misery and suffering and achieve peace and bliss.

MANTRAS # 12, # 13 and # 14:
MATERIAL AND SPIRITUAL KNOWLEDGE

Andhamtamah pravishyanti ye avidyam upasate.
Tato bhuya iva te tamo ya u vidyayam ratah. (# 12)

Ye	*upasate*	*avidyam*
Those,	who worship	material knowledge alone,

pravishyanti	*andhamtamah*
enter	deep darkness.

Ya u	*ratah*	*vidyayam*	*te*
Those who	delight in	spiritual knowledge alone,	they

tato bhuya iv	*tamo*
enter even greater	darkness.

Anyadeva ahur vidyayah anyad ahur avidyayah.
Iti shushruma dhiranam ye nastad vichachakshire. (# 13)

Ahur	*vidyayah*	*anyadeva*	*ahur*
It is said that	spiritual knowledge	has distinct results.	It is also said that

avidyayah	*anyad*	*Iti*	*shushruma*
material knowledge	has distinct results.	This	we have heard from

dhiranam	*ye*	*vichachakshire*	*nastad*
wise persons	who	have explained	these matters to us.

Vidyam cha avidyam cha yastad vedobhayam saha.
Avidyam mrityum titarva vidyaya amritam ashnute. (# 14)

Yas	*ved*	*tad obhyam saha*	*vidyam*
Those, who,	practice	side by side	spiritual knowledge

cha cha	*avidyam*
as well as	material knowledge,

titarva	*mrityum*	*avidyam*	*ashnute*
conquer	death	with material knowledge, and	attain

amritam	*vidyaya*
immortality	with spiritual knowledge.

DISCUSSION OF MANTRAS # 12, # 13, & # 14

The subject of mantras # 12, 13 and 14 is the significance of having spiritual knowledge as well as secular knowledge of the material world and physical universe. As has already been pointed out on page 16, the word *vidya* refers to spiritual knowledge, whereas the word *avidya* in the context of many Veda mantras, means secular knowledge of the material world (not ignorance as the word has sometimes been translated). Once again (like mantras # 9, 10 and 11) these three mantras as translated word for word from Sanskrit to English may seem paradoxical and confusing, but this is merely a device to emphasize both the similarities and the differences between *vidya* and *avidya*.

Mantra # 12 states that those persons who acquire knowledge of material things for personal grandeur or the exploitation of others or the environment may gain personal enrichment and gratification but will ultimately end up in deep misery. This group is made up of those people of whom one says, "A little knowledge is a dangerous thing" or of those who indiscriminately use the knowledge they have acquired without regard to the potential consequences (such as production of mass weapons).

Interestingly, the mantra later states that those who spend all of their energy acquiring spiritual knowledge live in even deeper ignorance and will end up in deeper misery. How is this apparently contrary conclusion possible? The reference here is to those who are clever in amassing a lot of spiritual information but have not adapted their lives to such knowledge or derived any wisdom from it (Rig Veda 10: 82: 7 and Yajur Veda 17: 31). Another mantra (Rig Veda 1: 164: 39) says that memorizing the Vedas is useless unless one realizes that they are about following God.

Such people are often given to the outward signs of religion (ritual, pomp, ceremony) without ever improving their souls. The message of this mantra is that the person who pretends to be a spiritual teacher but whose true focus is on the acquisition of power, wealth and fame is a fraud. He or she is a hypocrite and is in a far worse state than the person who openly pursues the acquisition of material things for personal gratification but does not pretend to do it in the name of God.

The next mantra, # 13, states that sages have long reflected over the relative merits of material versus spiritual knowledge and have come to the conclusion that each type of knowledge has both benefits and harmful outcomes depending upon how they are used. This mantra also implies that whenever one has difficulty with decisions, advice from gurus or other wise persons is essential.

The next mantra, # 14, says that both knowledge of spiritual things and practical secular knowledge can be great assets in life for the person who can master them for his own and humanity's benefit. Progress in the knowledge of material things (scientific progress) has clearly been useful both to the individual and to the society. Benefits, such as improved food production to decrease world hunger, better medical care to enhance and prolong life, are obvious examples. The mantra goes on to say that mastery of such knowledge helps one conquer death, which once again means misery in life. But material knowledge does not provide bliss and contentment. The acquisition of bliss and finding God requires the addition of spiritual knowledge and its practice in one's life. Spiritual knowledge and enlightenment comes from devotion to God, reading the Vedas and other scriptures, learning from a true guru or wise man, the performance of self-examination, the helping of others and the practice of yoga (meditation).

MANTRA # 15:
HOW TO LIVE UNTIL THE END OF LIFE

Vayur anilam amritam athedam bhasmantam shariram.
Om krato smara kilve smara kritam smara.

Vayur	*anilam*	*amritam*
The soul is always doing deeds.	It is not made up of physical matter.	It is immortal.

ath	*edam*	*shariram*	*bhasmantam*
On the other hand,	this,	body	turns to ashes.

Krato	*Om smara*
O human being, ceaseless performer,	always remember Almighty God.

kilve smara	*kritam smara*
Remember God to gain strength.	Remember God to perform your appropriate duties

DISCUSSION OF MANTRA # 15

This mantra describes the relationship between the physical body, the soul and God and gives advice on how one should live until the end of one's life. The mantra affirms that the soul is immortal; the soul does not contain physical matter and does not die with the death of the physical body. The soul has conscious energy and is always active performing one or the other karma. It is the soul that keeps us alive. At the time of the death of our physical body, depending on our karma, God gives our soul a new body and this cycle continues until moksha is obtained.

The body, on the other hand, contains physical matter and is prone to destruction and disintegration. This physical body that we spend hours on: meeting its need for food, decorating it and providing it with sensual pleasures is nothing without the soul and will rot without it. It arose from ashes (physical matter) and will end in ashes (either by cremation or burial).

The mantra next addresses the soul as the ceaseless performer of one or the other deeds and reminds it to always remember God,

OM. "God alone is your Protector and Master and your goal is to reach Him and not to focus on physical pleasures. Remember God to gain strength. Whenever you are discouraged, remember God your Protector and Benefactor, and your troubles will disappear. You will find the courage and strength to go on and will feel revitalized." It then says to the soul, "Remember God while doing your deeds. God will help you find the difference between virtuous and bad deeds and will guide you along the right path."

Mantra # 16:
PRAYER FOR LIVING A VIRTUOUS LIFE
AND OBTAINING GOD'S GRACE

Agne naya supatha raye asman vishvani deva vayunani vidvan.
Yuyodhyasmaj juhuranam eno bhuyishthan te nama uktim vidhema.

Agne	*naya asman*	*supatha*	*raye*
Luminous God, Our Ultimate Leader	lead us to the	right and noble path	to obtain prosperity and Thy grace.

Deva	*vidvan*	*vishvani vayunani*
Supreme Being,	You know	every one and all our deeds.

Yuyodhyasmaj	*juhuranam*	*eno*	*te*
Please help us remove from ourselves,	devious habits and	sins.	Dear god

nama uktim vidhema	*bhuyishthan*
we thank You and praise You	in our deepest regard.

DISCUSSION OF MANTRA # 16

This mantra reminds us that it is God alone who is our ultimate leader and we must pray only to God for guidance. The word *Agne* refers to God, the Ultimate Leader who leads us forward or the Power that helps us rise higher in life. It is because of this quality that the word *agne* or *agni* in the physical world is used to denote fire. Fire has the power to bring out the manifold characteristics of an object. For example, spices in a spice bottle have only a faint odor, but when roasted in the fire or used in cooking fill the house with their fragrance. Similarly, a person has more success when he makes God his leader instead of another human. The word *agne* in this mantra does not mean *fire god* as it has been sometimes called because of mistranslation.

The mantra then says, "Oh, our Supreme Leader, we pray to You that You may guide us, always reminding us to stay on the path of virtue. When we find failure in our lives, when we are in darkness, O luminous God, may You be the Light to guide us so that we do not follow the path of temptation. Dear God, bless us with both material and spiritual wealth." In the Vedas, both wealth and prosperity are actually encouraged so long as they are honestly achieved. The acquisition of wealth and prosperity requires that one not get attached to it. One is to be generous and have the responsibility of sharing it with those less fortunate; see page 31 for details. "While enjoying our physical wealth may we never forget You. May we always remain steadfast in our pursuit of You and find Your grace, peace and bliss. You, Supreme Lord, are omniscient and know all our deeds; none of our karmas are hidden from You. Dear God, You know we are far from being perfect and have many weaknesses and vices and are falling victims to various new temptations in life. Please help us to remove these vices from ourselves. Dear God, whenever we deviate from the righteous path, be our inner voice and remind us and guide us so that we not become the victims of vice and sin. Help us to abandon the old, crooked sinful ways and adopt virtuous ways in our lives. Dear God, for all Your blessings and loving-kindnesses to us, we thank You from the bottom of our hearts in every way possible. We praise You, we bow before You, we give You our homage and greetings so that we may always remain Your humble servants." (See pages 55–68 for details on prayer).

Mantra # 17:
A FINAL REMINDER: REACHING GOD
IS THE GOAL; DO NOT GO ASTRAY

Hiranmayena patrena satyasyapihitam mukham.
Yo asaavaditye purushah so asaavaham. Om Kham Brahm.

Hiranmayena patrena	*apihitam*	*satyasya mukham*
A golden lid or vessel	often covers or hides	the face of, or real truth.

Yo purushah	*asaav*	*aditye*	*so asaavaham*
God, the Supreme Being,	is	the Eternal Source of all Energy and	is present in every soul.

Om	*Kham*	*Brahm*
God	like space is all pervading,	and God is the Greatest.

DISCUSSION OF MANTRA # 17

This is the last mantra in the Yajur Veda, and the final reminder that the ultimate purpose of life is to reach God and find bliss and not to go astray in the journey called life. The mantra begins by telling us that if we get distracted or absorbed by the glitter that we see around us, then the real truth and purpose of life will become hidden. There are so many exciting and pleasurable attractions available to us (pursuit of money, power, sex, fame, special foods and entertainment, etc.) that we can easily squander all our energy in chasing our desires and giving in to our temptations. As we strive to fulfill our desires, we find we crave even more. It is then that we lose sight of God, our real spiritual goal, and make little spiritual progress in life.

The second line of the mantra states that, in order to obtain moksha, one must remember that God alone is the Eternal Source of all Energy in the universe. God is indestructible. God is the Supreme Being, the Supreme Consciousness, the Ultimate Reality. The word *Aham* signifies God, the Universal SELF, the Universal Spirit that is present in every soul and everywhere in the universe. In common Sanskrit usage, however, *Aham* also means *I, me* or my individual self. (Notice the difference between SELF = God and self = me. See Mandookya Upanishad by Swami Satyam for details.) Some authors have translated the three words *so assav aham* as "I am the same as God."

As stated earlier on page 27, the conscious energy of the soul is very limited when compared to God. Therefore, the soul (*Atma*) never becomes *Paramatma* (the Supreme Soul or Spirit) that stands for God alone. When one attains moksha the soul becomes close to or aligns with God but never truly becomes God. Every soul, on the other hand, can and should strive to acquire some of God's qualities such as kindness, justice and love towards others.

The last three words of the Yajur Veda, **Om Kham Brahm,** remind the reader (or the listener) that the essence of the Vedas is that one should always remember OM (God), because God is the Greatest; there is no other power that equals Him. And God is present everywhere; He fills all space. Meditate on Om, and hear the resonance of Om in both the mind and soul. Pray to God alone and follow no message but His. If you live in this way, you will find God's grace and bliss.

Section III

YOGA

The word yoga (yōgə which is pronounced without the final a as yog) means the union of the soul with God. Yoga is a path of personal spiritual development that utilizes meditation to bring enlightenment, self-realization and, ultimately, the attainment of God and bliss. While yoga is primarily a spiritual method, it includes attention to physical and mental well-being as well. The practice of yoga teaches how to turn the senses and the mind away from their usual areas of interest in outside things and other such distractions—so the mind can focus inward, become tranquil, and allow experience deep meditation.

Unfortunately, as stated previously, the word yoga has been rather misused in the West. For many people, yoga means various physical exercises, postures, and contortions of the body aimed at promoting good health, reducing stress and relaxing the body, as well as possibly alleviating physical ailments in a natural way without the use of drugs or medications. Many practitioners of yoga will also include control of the breathing or other breathing exercises as part of yoga. A select few will go further and include meditation and/or concentration of the mind as a part of yoga. Yoga, however, is much more than that. Yoga is an integral part of the Vedic Hindu religion with the ultimate goal of attaining union with God. In the previous two sections, in several places, it was stated that God resides even inside the soul. This would imply that the soul is already united with God. The purpose of yoga is to make the soul **conciously aware** of God, the Supreme Being, Supreme Consciousness and Supreme Bliss so that the soul may be enlightened and attain bliss.

Yoga has been an integral part of the Vedic Hindu religion from time immemorial. Various aspects of yoga have been discussed in both the Vedas and Upanishads in several places (Yajur Veda 11:1–5 and 31: 18; Mandookya Upanishad and Kathopanishad). As has been already pointed out, the original recording of the Vedas (see pages 41–44) are believed to have been accomplished by seers (rishis) while in samadhi, that superconscious state where the mind is completely tranquil so that God and His knowledge may be directly revealed to the soul.

For a considerable period of time the practice of yoga was passed on orally from gurus to their pupils. Somewhat later, rishi Patanjali organized the practice of yoga in a systematic manner, as the Yoga Darshana (yoga aphorisms), which constitutes one of the six Darshanas. (See pages 47–50.)

There are four principal types of yoga:

1. Raj yoga, also called Dhyana yoga, Meditation yoga, Royal yoga or the eight-step yoga
2. Karma yoga, the yoga of action and selfless deeds
3. Jnana (also spelled Gyana) yoga, the yoga of spiritual knowledge
4. Bhakti yoga, the yoga of devotion

RAJ YOGA (also called DHYANA YOGA, the yoga of meditation or concentration): This yoga follows the eight progressive steps described by the seer Patanjali and is sometimes called *ashtanga* (the eight-step) yoga. As part of the eight steps, it incorporates the other three yogas (Karma, Jnana and Bhakti) in it, but the main emphasis is upon the concentration of the mind and meditation as the means of achieving samadhi leading to self-realization as well as the attainment of God and bliss.

KARMA YOGA: This yoga is devoted to the performance of actions (karma), which are selfless and in the service of God. Karmas of this sort do not bind a person to his actions, but rather liberate him or her toward God. In the final stages of this yoga, all of the actions performed are in the service of God. This includes such mundane activities as eating and sleeping because these actions allow the person to live longer and continue to serve others. They are not merely for personal benefit or gratification.

JNANA (GYANA) YOGA: This yoga is concerned with the acquisition of spiritual knowledge and wisdom and incorporating them into one's life. This involves recognizing God as the Creator of the Universe, the Almighty, Omnipotent, Omnipresent and Omniscient One and the Source of all spiritual knowledge. The knowledge obtained through this yoga is called viveka (also see page 16) and helps a person understand the true nature of God, soul and prakriti. This enlightenment enables the soul to break attachments to material things and make effort to attain God through meditation.

BHAKTI YOGA: This yoga is based upon complete devotion and surrender to God. The devotee discovers the glory of God reflected in every aspect of living and in every part of the universe. Once the Glory and Unity of God in all things are perceived, the aspirant praises God and sings His glory, receiving grace in return. It is important that the devotee not ask for anything of material value because God's judgment and mercy will provide these to the true believer.

These four different yogas are not mutually exclusive. They, in fact, complement one another and incorporate one or more aspects of the other yogas into their practice. The choice of which yoga to follow belongs to the aspirant. All human beings are by nature different one from the other; some will be more inclined to choose one path over another. Some people are more action oriented, others seek more knowledge, and there are those who want to express more devotion. Of these four yogas, Raj Yoga is the best organized and requires the most discipline, so if one makes a sincere effort to pursue it, one is least likely to go astray. Therefore, the remainder of this section will focus on Raj Yoga as described by Patanjali.

THE RAJ YOGA OF PATANJALI

Patanjali's Yog-Darshan contains 195 surtras (aphorisms) divided into four chapters to describe the various aspects of yoga. The pervading theme throughout is that the purpose of yoga is to make the mind tranquil so that one can meditate deeply in order to obtain enlightenment, reach God and find bliss. The chapters successively describe the methods of advancing in the practice of yoga as well as the hindrances that are commonly encountered. The emphasis in each of the four chapters is nevertheless different.

Chapter I: Samadhi Pada

This chapter begins with a definition of yoga and classifies the various states of mind ranging from confusion and agitation to resolution and tranquility. Next follows a discussion of the natural inclinations and distractions of the mind (both good and bad); the means for overcoming them so that the mind may become tranquil; advancement in yoga practices; and ultimately, the attainment of the superconscious state of samadhi. The emphasis in this chapter is on the description of the various stages of samadhi and the means for the acquisition of knowledge of the true nature of the soul as well as the advancement toward God and bliss. This chapter contains 51 aphorisms.

Chapter II: Sadhana Pada

This chapter describes the means (*sadhana* in Sanskrit) for advancing in the practice of yoga and the spiritual, mental and physical benefits that the practitioner gains. The aphorisms in the first part of the chapter begin with a general description of the various methods and then cover the first five steps of the eight-step yoga in considerable detail. This chapter contains 55 aphorisms.

Chapter III: Vibhooti Pada

This chapter begins by discussing the last three steps of the eight-step yoga. The emphasis is on the extraordinary abilities or powers (*vibhooti*) acquired by an accomplished yogi as advancement proceeds. It is somewhat hard to decipher the extent of these abilities, as well as determine how much of the description is symbolic versus actual physical and/or mental accomplishment. Some of the vibhootis described are: the power to recall the past and foretell the future to some extent; the ability to recall some aspects of previous births (incarnations); the capacity to know what others are thinking; the acquisition of great physical strength like that of an elephant; the ability to withstand thirst and hunger for a prolonged period; the aptitude to gain knowledge easily in any chosen field; the acquisition of knowledge about planets and the stars (cosmos); and many other powers.

The chapter also has an admonition that although the yogi may acquire many extraordinary powers, they should not lead to temptation or vanity (Yoga 3: 37 and 51). The yogi must accept these powers with humility and with the desire of helping others in a selfless manner. He or she must never challenge God's authority or abuse the powers in such a way as to bring harm to others. The public display or flaunting of such powers is strongly discouraged, because these extraordinary abilities can also become hindrances rather than assets. The display of yogic powers in the manner of a magician is not only frowned upon but may lead to the downfall of the yogi. There are 55 aphorisms in this chapter.

Chapter IV: Kaivalyam Pada

This chapter is concerned with salvation (the attainment of God and moksha). The word kaivalyam means attainment of Divine Consciousness, a dispassionate state in which all of the bonds of the soul to material things have been removed, and the soul is free to be with God in a state of immense bliss. There are 34 aphorisms in this chapter.

Although it might be desirable to translate each individual aphorism word for word from the Sanskrit and then discuss each aphorism in some detail, as was done previously with the mantras from the Yajur Veda in Section II, such a project is beyond the limited scope of this book. In addition, understanding the translation of each aphorism depends upon a detailed familiarity with the content of the Vedic Hindu scriptures. Without it the aphorisms are hard to follow. This book aims to give an introduction to the more salient aspects of yoga, rather than providing a detailed discussion. Some reference books that include the translation and interpretation of each of the aphorisms are provided at the end of this book.

The discussion of Patanjali s Yoga that follows is divided into two subsections. Subsection # 1 includes translations and discussions of the first four aphorisms from the first chapter of Patanjali s book because they describe in a condensed form the purpose and general nature of yoga. This subsection also includes the concept of mind as used by Patanjali and in other Vedic writings. Subsection # 2 includes a description of the most important precepts of yoga; these provide a continuing theme for all four chapters. Thereafter follows a detailed discussion of the eight-step yoga.

SUBSECTION #1: The first four aphorisms and the description of mind

Aphorism # 1: Atha yoga anushasnam.

Atha (here is a discourse on) *yoga anushasnam* (the discipline of yoga).

The Sanskrit word *atha* in Vedic scriptures is used at the beginning of a text and implies that the discourse is for the benefit and well-being of the reader and mankind. The emphasis in this aphorism is on the word discipline, because no advancement in yoga is possible without discipline. The most important element is a strong commitment to follow the eight steps of yoga in a progressive manner. It would be unreasonable to expect success in the later steps if the first ones were ignored or treated lightly.

A commitment must be made to incorporate the first two steps of yoga into one s life on a 24-hour basis each day. For the remaining six steps, the duration of practice begins small and gradually increases. It is said that progress in yoga is easy for certain aspirants. The reason may be based upon their deep faith in and devotion to God, as well as the sum result of their karma in this and previous lives. However, most persons initially find following the steps of yoga to be a very slow and difficult adventure. Many either simply give up or spend time searching for short cuts. This aphorism reminds us that discipline and practice are essential for progress.

Sustained practice in yoga is called *abhyasa*. Instructions from a guru whose life reflects yoga teachings is both desirable and very helpful, but it is not absolutely essential for progress, should no guru be available. Aphorism 1: 26 reminds us that guru of all gurus is God. If no other guru is available, one can directly seek God's guidance.

Aphorism # 2: Yogas chitta vritti nirodha.

Yogas (yoga is), *nirodha* (stopping or removing), *chitta* (mind's), *vritti* (those activities or inclinations that cause agitation of the mind).

The second aphorism of Patanjali's Yog-Darshan states that the purpose of yoga is to stop and finally uproot those activities, propensities and activities of the mind that cause agitation so that the mind can become tranquil and pass into a state of perfect peace.

The word *vritti* in yoga refers to activities and inclinations of the mind. The purpose of yoga is not to suppress the mind because, when suppressed, the mind's activities continue to smolder. Rather, the aim of yoga is to progress to a state of calmness where all of mind's usual distracting activities cease and the superconscious state of samadhi may be attained.

The activities of the mind in the Vedic Hindu scriptures are usually divided into five states ordered from the least to the most desirable:

1. Dull, inert, lazy, disinterested
2. Agitated, restless, indulgent
3. Active, interested and directed but without sustained resolve, easily distracted
4. Resolute, concentrated, pointed, focused
5. Tranquil, calm

These states of mind are mainly thought of in their spiritual context, but a secular interpretation is equally possible. Most persons exist in the first three states, especially in the second. However, none of these is fit for advancement in yoga. Real yoga begins when the mind is resolute (state 4) and becomes more established in state 5. Even when a person's mind exists mainly in states 4 and 5, it may be distracted. Every practitioner of yoga therefore (as stated earlier in aphorism # 1) needs both discipline and sustained practice (abhyasa).

Aphorism # 3: *Tada avasthanam drushtuh swarupe.*

Tada avasthanam (in that state the soul abides in) **drushtuh swarupe** (its essential form of spirit as well as in the Supreme Self or God).

The third aphorism describes what happens when the mind is made completely tranquil. The words *drushtuh swarupe* in this aphorism have been translated in two different ways, although the translations are not mutually exclusive but rather complementary. The first translation is, "The soul sees its true eternal self" as completely distinct from body and mind, free of all attachments to items made of matter (prakriti). This is the state of self-realization. This state is not, however, an end in itself. In the next stage, the soul remains steadfast on a one-to-one basis with God (the Supreme Self/Spirit, the Self who pervades even our soul). This manages to form the basis for the second translation, "The soul abides in the Supreme Soul" because it is only then (when the mind is completely tranquil) that the soul finds bliss in the Supreme Bliss, which is God alone (also see page 106).

Aphorism # 4: Vrittisarupyam itratra.

Itratra (In other states) *vrittisarupyam* (the mind is attracted to its indulgent activities, inclinations and tendencies).

This aphorism reminds us that each of us has a free will and choices to make in life's journey. It is certainly possible to indulge one's mind in the distractions of the material world and identify one's soul with the gratification of sensual pleasures. Unfortunately, the continued fulfilling of the mind's indulgent tendencies only leads to increased attachments and further bondage of the soul to the material world with the accompanying spiritual emptiness and profound unhappiness.

On the other hand, it is possible to choose the spiritual path of aphorism # 3, which leads to enlightenment, the attainment of God and immense bliss. For those desiring spiritual elevation, there is but one choice, the path of yoga. Sadly, only a few persons choose this avenue. As was noted earlier, the master yogi Krishna states in the Gita that there are only a small number of people in this world who are interested in a spiritual path and among them only a very few will pursue it in earnest. These people, however, are the only ones who will find bliss and salvation (see page 20).

DIFFERENT ASPECTS OF MIND AS DESCRIBED IN THE VEDIC SCRIPTURES

The English language defines the mind as that part of the human being that thinks, feels and wills. It is the center of all mental activity. But is the mind truly the center of all mental activity or is the soul? Several Vedic Hindu scriptures describe the soul as the final site of all perceptions and the executor of all decisions. Free will may only be exercised by the soul. Nevertheless, the soul is surrounded by the mind and must act through it. The soul is by nature conscious, while the mind is inert in and of itself. Only in conjunction with the soul can it carry out its usual activities of thinking, feeling and making decisions. There are prayers in the Vedas to ask for a resolute mind so that once the soul makes a sound decision, the mind does not weaken or falter.

In the future, the computer may develop to the extent that it functions more and more like a human mind. However, since it is composed of matter, it will never possess a soul or achieve the potential of a yogic mind.

When we are awake our minds are always active. Its activities can be either directed externally, focusing on what the senses perceive or internally, towards meditation and contemplation. The mind cannot perform both activities simultaneously, so it must always choose between them. Both activities are important. External activities help us to live in the world, and internal activities help us to realize who we are and reach God. Most people's minds are predominantly focused on external matters. When the mind is directed inward, as it is in the later stages of yoga, some special things begin to happen: The true nature of the eternal soul is perceived as separate from what is usually called "I" or "me" (these are attributes of the ego), and the true potential of the enlightened soul begins to be realized.

In the Vedic scriptures, the mind is often subdivided into either three or four interconnected parts. The Sanskrit word *antahkaran* is generally used as a generic word to include all aspects of the mind. At times, the words *mana* (also called *manas*), *chit* and *buddhi* may also be used to mean mind in the generic sense, rather than meaning designated parts of the mind. When the word antahkaran is used it implies the inclusion of *mana, ahankara, chit* and *buddhi;* although, in at least one system, chit and buddhi are viewed as combined and used interchangeably.

For the purpose of the present discussion, antahkaran will be seen as comprising four parts. Along with the soul, antahkaran is located in the brain but has outreach through neurological connections to the sense and action organs as well as to all parts of the body. In Vedic scriptures, antahkaran is viewed to exist in the brain in a subtle state in the form of neurological energy and not as gross brain tissue.

MANA: (mun'ə, pronounced mun) Mana is that part of antahkaran that is in contact with the external world from which it receives messages by means of the five senses. In its usual state, mana is restless and agitated. When one is awake, mana tries to receive messages from the exterior as well as from past memories. It processes the messages in conjunction with input from the other three components of antahkaran and then from the soul. Next, mana executes the response of the soul in conjunction with antahkaran by means of the action organs. It also has the option of getting further sensory input before making a final response. Because all of our external responses are executed by mana, the final resolutions or will power of the soul will be executed by this means as well. The free will of the soul is executed by means of the mana. Sometimes mana is seen as divided into two parts: the *deva* portion, which receives the input of the senses and the *yaksha* part, which executes the responses through the action organs.

CHIT and *BUDDHI:* In some Vedic scriptures these two components of antahkaran are described as separate entities, while in others they are combined into a single item called chit as in Patanjali's Yog Darshan or buddhi as in Kapil's Sankhya Darshan. While the following discussion treats them as separate entities, it must be recognized that they are intricately intertwined and are often thought of as one.

CHIT (or chitum): This is that part of antahkaran, which is the seat of our feelings, emotions and desires. It is the place in the mind where anger and/or kindness; hate and/or love; fear and/or bravery are aroused. When we hear someone say, "I like it" or "I want it," it is in the chit component of the mind that these wants, desires, likes, cravings, greed and avarice are expressed. Chit is that part of the mind that gives us attachment to material things and makes us think possessively about our relationships, rather than allowing them to be enriching and liberating. On the other hand, chit is also the site of our feelings of being generous and caring.

Common expression of feelings such as, "This comes from the heart," "I love you from the bottom of my heart" or "Have a heart" all belong to chit. Do these feelings really come from our heart or do they come from our brain? Modern science tells us that these feelings come from the brain, and that the use of the word *heart* is not only poetic but also a vestige of the past. Despite this knowledge, no one says, "I love you from the bottom of my brain."

Likewise, there is considerable controversy about the location of chit. Some yoga teachers, especially those who follow Hatha yoga, describe chit as being located in the heart, buddhi in the brain and antahkaran in both. They also believe that the soul normally resides in the heart surrounded by chit but must rise to the brain through the practice of yoga in order to achieve salvation and enlightenment. Other yoga teachers and scholars clearly place the soul and chit in that part of the brain that has close connections with the heart and insist that the use of the word "heart" (as the physical heart in the chest) is a misreading of the Vedic scriptures.

According to the latter group, the word heart is symbolic of that vital core of the brain that is essential for our survival. The exact site for chit, according to modern neuroanatomy that would correspond to Vedic scriptures, is hard to be clear about. It is not clear where "the heart felt feelings" come from in the brain, whether they are in the cingulate cortex, limbic system, hypothalamus or come from numerous anatomic sites of the brain. Further, modern science is not at present completely sure how emotions affect the heart; whether they are expressed by neural connections, by means of hormones, by both or by some as yet unknown mechanism or combination of mechanisms.

Lastly, chit is also the seat of our remote memory and our subconscious memories. The root impressions of all our previous deeds and experiences both in this life and from past incarnations exist in a dormant state. These lasting impressions are called *sanskars* (also spelled *samskaras*) in the Vedic scriptures. God not only judges us on the basis of each karma we perform but also on the intent of that karma called karmashya. (Also see page 85.)

Each karma and its karmashya leave a lasting impression in our chit. The most significant ones become our sanskars. Chit is the place where these sanskars periodically activate and become expressed as overt desires, cravings and emotions.

Everyone is born with pre-formed sanskars (based upon karmas from previous lives) and adds new sanskars, which are established by present and future karmas. Our previously formed sanskars influence what karmas we perform at present. But if our free will is exercised properly, especially if there is good input from the intellect, there is allowance for the performance of new and better karmas. Our future conduct is not etched in stone or is daily life predetermined. (See pages 27–33 and 80–85.)

Chit, then, can be activated both by rekindling our old sanskars and by new information provided from our senses via the *mana*. All activities that cause an agitation of the chit (desires, strong emotions, attachments) are called vrittis (see page 115). Patanjali's Yog Darshan (2: 3–9) identifies five vrittis that are called *klistha*, because they cause pain and suffering as well as agitation of the mind. They are ignorance, arrogance (prompted by vanity), indulgent attachments (those that bind), jealousy and/or hate, and fear (especially the fear of death). It is possible to suppress these five vrittis for a period of time, but they continue to rekindle and express themselves until they are overcome.

The purpose of yoga is first to modify those vrittis that agitate the mind to virtuous vrittis that do not agitate the mind but bring peace and happiness instead. These virtuous vrittis are called *aklishta* (as opposed to *klishta*) and consist of such things as spiritual knowledge; kindness and forgiveness; generosity and unselfishness; love, caring and compassion; fearlessness and bravery.

Although, it is very desirable to have aklishta vrittis instead of klishta vrittis, every yoga aspirant must remember that when the virtuous vrittis are performed with a desire for something in return or a reward, they are still vrittis because they do not uproot attachments or vanity or make the mind tranquil. Virtue must be pursued for virtue alone. It is only by meditating and doing selfless deeds without thought of reward that the old sankars are uprooted and the mind becomes tranquil. This is how the soul is directed towards self-realization, reaching God and attaining bliss.

BUDDHI: Buddhi means intellect and is that component of antahkaran that helps us analyze information, determine what is good or bad and decide between right and wrong. It assists in thinking and in remembering things at a conscious level. It is the site of conscious memory. Buddhi interacts with the other three components of antahkaran, the information brought by mana, the activities of chit and the functions of ahankara and presents its analyses for the soul to exercise its will power. Buddhi has been divided into four levels in the Vedic scriptures:

Ordinary buddhi: the basic level of intelligence possessed by all human beings (previously described; see page 17).

Dhee: the level of the intellect that discriminates right from wrong. Dhee is acquired by practicing dharma or the first four steps of yoga (see page 17).

Medha: the activation of the brain's concentrating and analyzing abilities. Medha is developed as a result of the practice of Steps 5 through 7 of the eight-step yoga (see pages 140–144) where one's concentrating and analyzing abilities are highly activated. It is here that the understanding of the nature of the antahkaran begins and the recognition that the soul is separate from the anhatkaran is developed. Now one can acquire any knowledge one desires very easily.

Prajna (also spelled Pragya): the highest level of intellect that can only be acquired through samadhi, the eighth and final step of yoga (see pages 143–144) where God's knowledge is revealed directly to the soul (Yoga 1: 48–51). This is the state the rishis were in when the Vedas were revealed.

AHANKARA: Ahankara is that part of antahkaran that gives us personal identity. Personal identity is what helps us take responsibility for whatever we do, such as meet our daily needs, help raise a family and do our share for the society. Therefore, ahankara is essential for individual survival, but ahankara very often turns into our possessive nature that identifies with "I," "Me," "Mine," our ego. When a person says, "This is my child," what does she mean? Does the child really belong to the parent? Or does the child belong to himself and the parent only the temporary guardian? When ahankara is not properly bridled it leads to vanity, narcissm, selfishness, jealousy and self-centeredness. It is thus that ahankara, like chit's klishta vrittis, can impede the liberation of the soul.

In order for self-realization to occur, the ego must be replaced with humility. In order to subdue the ego, it is necessary to understand that everything in the universe ultimately belongs to God and that we are, at best, its temporary caretakers. Once the physical body dies, we take nothing with us but the consequences of our karma. It is, therefore, essential to develop non-attachment to worldly possessions. In a like manner, all human relationships are transitory. This does not mean that we have no ties to those we love or have no responsibilities toward them, but it does exclude possessiveness in relationships. (Also see page 30.)

The nature of the soul is identical in all living beings. It is only our deeds and the physical covering that makes us appear different. The fully realized person sees the unity of God in all living things and develops universal love for them. (Also see pages 90–92.)

The following story might help clarify the various aspects of anhatkaran. An obese man finds he has a high cholesterol count and heart disease with periodic chest pain (exertional angina). He is intelligent and knows that in addition to his medications he must lose weight and modify his diet. He begins to do this. One day he goes to the mall and sees and smells fudge being made. The sight and smell of the fudge are delivered to his mana. His buddhi recalls that fudge tastes delicious, but also reminds his self (soul) that the fudge may have been okay to eat when he was young, it is no longer good for him and he must avoid eating it. His chit rekindles his childhood memories and emotions associated with fudge. He remembers his parents taking him to the county fair where he had a big piece of very delicious homemade fudge. Now if the chit were calm it would tell the soul to act according to buddhi and avoid eating the fudge. If, on the other hand, the chit were excited and had a craving for fudge, it would try to cajole the man into trying the fudge with a statement like, "Well, a little piece wouldn't hurt, would it?" The man's buddhi again reminds him that the fudge is bad for his health. Now his ahankara enters the debate and tells him, "Don't be so hard on yourself! You can handle it. A little piece won't do any harm." It is now the time for the self (soul) to synthesize all the input from the various parts of the antahkaran and decide how to use its free will. If the chit is agitated and the desire for fudge out of hand and the ego is out of control, then the man will be persuaded to use his action organs to get the fudge. On the other hand, if the chit is calm and the ego under control, the man may fondly remember his childhood experience but will ultimately exercise wisdom and avoid eating the fudge.[1]

While it is true that the soul is the final master of the body, in most of us the soul often functions as a slave to the antahkaran. The mind can be activated by external stimuli brought in via the mana, as well as from within by the chit, or ahankara based on old sanskars. The mana, chit and ahankara each try to impose their message on the soul for fulfillment. Our buddhi (intellect), on the other hand, when working well reminds us of right and wrong, telling us what will enlighten our soul and what will be self-

---

[1]This story has been modified from a story I heard several years ago at one of Swami Satyam's lectures.

destructive. The buddhi does not impose itself on the soul; it merely offers counsel. The soul, being conscious, must exercise its will power and reclaim its position as master of the mind. In the movie "Star Wars," OB Wan (Ben Kanobe) while training Luke Skywalker to become a Jedi warrior and learn the use of his weapon says, "Let go of your feelings (your ego). Let the force be your guide." This could be interpreted as meaning, "When you get rid of all distractions from the chit, your soul and buddhi is free to concentrate and learn from God." The purpose of yoga is to overcome the soul's habitual alignment with the activities of mana, chit and/or ahankar and, with practice, gradually align itself with the highest order of buddhi known as prajna where the soul receives direct knowledge from God.

Subsection # 2:
The Most Salient Precepts of Yoga and the Eight-Step Yoga

This subsection begins with a description of the main precepts of yoga that form the basis for a continuing theme throughout all four chapters and include the following:

Eeshwar Pranidhan:	Surrender to God
Shradha:	Faith and Devotion Based on Truth
Prarthana:	Prayer
Anushasnam and Abhyasa:	Discipline and Practice
Vairagya:	Dispassion and Renunciation

Eeshwar (also spelled *Ishwara*) *Pranidhan:*
This Sanskrit phrase literally means complete surrender to God. It makes clear that reaching God is the primary goal of life and that every other aim is completely subordinate to this objective. Such surrender does not imply the passive acceptance of fate, a life of inaction or the rote performance of dogmatic rituals. Quite the contrary, *Eeshwar pranidhan* demands active

participation, which is to be expressed by the dedication of all of a person's actions in a selfless manner to the service of God without any desire whatsoever for any kind of return or personal gratification. Once this karma is performed, whatever God gives in return is joyfully accepted without any hint of complaint. Such a person views God's universe as full and complete and expresses his faith in prayers such as, "God, thy will be done." This is one of the most important aphorisms of Patanjali's Yoga Sutras and is clearly emphasized in four of the 195 aphorisms (1: 23, 2: 1, 2: 32 and 2: 45).

Eeshwar pranidhan represents the final goal of each of the four yogas—Raj, Jnana, Bhakti and Karma. A person who can completely surrender to God has no personal worries or desires left. His or her mind is devoid of all agitation (vrittis) and becomes tranquil and, with God's grace finds enlightenment, inner peace and bliss. This is the essence of all yoga. For a person in whom Eeshwar pranidhan exists intensely, he or she directly progresses to the eighth step of the eight-step yoga.

SHRADHA: The Sanskrit word shradha usually implies a deep abiding faith in God coupled with ceaseless devotion to God. The literal interpretation of shradha is based upon its root words shrat (truth) and dha (adopt into one's life). Therefore, it means adopting and following truth in all aspects of one's life at all times. This idea contains the implication that faith in and devotion to God must always be based upon divine truth. There is no place here for blind faith or devotion to the followings of a charismatic teacher or guru. When an individual's faith in and devotion to God has become so intense that the Glory of God is seen in every aspect of the universe and that every moment of life is spent in seeking God, then the individual will attain God. This is the essence of Bhakti yoga. The precept of shradha is emphasized in aphorisms 1: 20 and 1: 21.

PRARTHANA: This Sanskrit word means prayer. It has been previously stated in the section on prayer that God does not need our flattery. (See pages 55–59 for details.) Prayers are to give thanks to God for all His (or Her) kindnesses to us and for reminding us that the attainment of God is the primary goal of life and that virtuous living is the means of attaining this goal. In yoga, prayer emanates as a continuation of *eeshwar pranidhan* and *shradha*. Aphorisms 1: 27 and 1: 28 state that to advance in yoga and make the mind tranquil one should perform a silent chant (called *japa*) of God's name OM while contemplating that God alone is omnipresent, omnipotent and omniscient, and seeking God's grace with faith and devotion.

ANUSHASNAM and *ABHYASA*: These words mean discipline and sustained practice respectively. It has already been stated (see pages 114–115) that yoga must be seen as a commitment in all aspects of one's life. Progress is dependent upon persistent effort and vigilance. It becomes ceaseless devotion and the desire to follow yoga in every aspect of one's life. There will be setbacks and no sudden transformations. But with continued practice progress is certain. Great is the effort and great the reward. These two precepts are emphasized in aphorisms 1: 1; 1: 12–14 and 2: 47.

VAIRAGYA and *PARAM VAIRAGYA:* The word vairagya means dispassion, renunciation and a detachment from possessiveness in combination. In no way does it imply running away from one's responsibilities. Rather, it demands meeting all worldly responsibilities according to the rules of dharma. First, vairagya requires both commitment and effort to detach from worldly possessions. A person who decides to stop cheating or taking bribes is not incorporating vairagya into his or her life, rather he or she is just beginning to walk the path of virtue (dharma).

The next task is moving away from possessive bondages with close relatives, one's children or spouse. You no longer speak of them as **my** child or **my** partner, since such persons do not really belong to you. The goal in these close relationships is to meet the responsibilities with love and care and to help them along their own path towards God. Finally, as one advances to intense renunciation and dispassion (called param vairagya), then the only effort in life becomes the pursuit of God. Such a person has no bondages left and the whole world becomes his or her home and family. (The person is a true Sanyasi; see page 40.) Such a person finds God's love and glory everywhere. Vairagya is therefore a continuation of *eeshwar pranidhan* in a different format. These precepts are emphasized in aphorisms 1: 12, 1: 15 and 1:16.

Mahatma Anand Swami Ji used to relate the following story about vairagya.

One day, while learning and practicing yoga in Uttarkashi (in the Himalayas near the source of the Ganges) he met a sanyasi who was weeping. He asked the sanyasi what was the matter. The sanyasi replied that he had no physical ailments but that he was very sad. He was thinking about his wife and children and the comforts of a home that he had left a few years previously following a quarrel. He sorely missed his home and family. Mahatma Anand Swami Ji laughed a little and then said, "Dear man, to become a sanyasi is not a punishment or a burden of life that you must bear. Old sanskars (latent memories) do occasionally flare up even in a sanyasi, but you do have to make a choice. As a sanyasi you must either make the whole world your home and family or you must give up being a sanyasi, go back home to your family, become a householder again and live a virtuous life. You must remain a sanyasi only if your soul and mind are into it."

THE EIGHT-STEP YOGA

The eight steps of yoga are as follows:

I *YAMA:* Self control, abstention from vices

II *NIYAMA:* Moral practices and discipline

III *AASANA:* Postures for the practice of yoga

IV *PRANAYAMA:* Control of the breathing and the body's vital energy

V *PRATYAHARA:* Withdrawal of the mind from sensory stimuli

VI *DHARANA:* Concentration

VII *DHYANA:* Deep meditation

VIII *SAMADHI:* The superconscious state of enlightenment

STEPS I and II: YAMA and NIYAMA

The word yama in yogic parlance means self-control in the conduct of life with emphasis on refraining from vices. The word niyama refers to the various moral disciplines of life that must be observed in order to progress further in yoga. Because these two are interrelated, they are being discussed together. In fact, there are five yamas and five niyamas that will be described in detail. It will soon become obvious that several yamas and niyamas are either the same as or very similar to the 10 virtuous acts included previously in the definition of dharma (see pages 10–22). This is the means by which yoga and dharma are linked to each other.

The focus of yoga in the West has been expressed in exercises that are contained in step three (Aasana) of the eight-step yoga. The first two steps, yama and niyama, are almost totally ignored. Nevertheless, genuine yoga teachers in India have always strongly emphasized that mastering the first two steps is absolutely essential for any type of advancement in yoga practice, no matter how useful the exercises may be for health. It is in these first two steps that the pupil begins to learn to concentrate the mind away from distractions, which is necessary to accomplish deep meditation.

The five yamas are as follows:

1. *AHIMSA (or AHINSA):* Nonviolence, absence of doing harm

The usual English translation of the word ahimsa is nonviolence, but the word actually implies the replacement of cruelty and killing and with love, compassion and forgiveness. Ahimsa demands controlling our tendencies to be angry with and do harm to others. The word nonviolence has often ended up implying being passive or powerless, lacking sufficient strength to fight back. Quite the contrary, ahimsa is an act of courage, a commitment to avoid hurting, fighting with or killing others in thought word and deed and is an attribute of the strong and brave. Ahimsa does not mean avoiding the fight against injustice, but rather the fighting of injustice by nonviolent means whenever possible. Also, ahimsa does not mean that one should just "take it" when attacked and not fight back, although it forbids attacking and harming others for personal pleasure or advantage.

The idea of being a vegetarian in the Vedic Hindu religion is based upon the concept of ahimsa, the avoidance of bringing harm and death to animals when food needs could be met by other nonviolent means.

One of the most difficult things to achieve in life is the overcoming of doing harm at the level of thought. How is it possible to accomplish this? This is only possible when the soul of every other being is seen to be the same as one's own soul; when there is true brotherly love for others. When anyone deliberately tries to harm us, we usually develop a sense of enmity toward that person and start to plan retaliation, which often involves violence. By learning compassion and forgiveness and treating others with love and kindness, it is possible to overcome violence: it takes two to fight. A yoga aspirant must gradually learn to behave in a saintly manner. This is the type of ahimsa spoken of by Buddha and Mahatma Gandhi and the brotherly love of Christ. The punishment of the sinner or evil doer belongs to God, not to the yoga student.

All that has been said about ahimsa refers to behavior on the personal level. Ahimsa does not forbid the state from punishing a criminal or a nation from fighting back when attacked or when its security is threatened. In the Gita, Krishna (a master yogi) advises the brave warrior Arjuna on his duty to kill and vanquish the evil Kuru brothers who had repeatedly refused to resolve their differences by just and peaceful means.

2. *SATYA:* Truth (previously discussed in conjunction with dharma; see pages 17 18).

3. *ASTEYA:* Not coveting (previously discussed; see page 15).

4. *BRAHMACHARYA:* Chastity

The word brahmacharya literally means all conduct in life that promotes a feeling of being close to God. The emphasis in the Vedic scriptures has always been on being chaste in thought, word and action. It is impossible to be a slave to sex and keep the mind tranquil. According to Manu and others, brahmacharya has meant being celibate in three of the four ashramas. (See pages 38 41.) Only those who were householders and belonged to the Grahastha ashrama were expected to have sex with the goal of procreation. This is the type of behavior that was expected of those who wanted to follow the path of yoga and ultimately reach God. A yoga aspirant in following brahmachyra is expected to sublimate his or her sexual desires into spiritual energy and perform all karma in the service of God.

In the Vedic Hindu scriptures it has been recognized that accomplishing strict brahmachyra is a very difficult task and most people will not succeed. However, making an effort to follow it is mandatory for progress in yoga.

It should now be clear that yoga is not for the improvement of sexual techniques and practices as some yoga teachers in the West claim. In the past (and present), both in India and in the West, there have been several self-proclaimed gurus who have preached that following the practices of dharma and yoga are nonsense and that one should be free to indulge in all of life s pleasures including sex without restraint. Erotic art, such as that seen at the Khajuraho temples and erotic love manuals like the Kama Sutra, are also part of Hindu culture but have no place in the practice of yoga.

5. *APRIGRAHA:* Non-possessiveness, control of desires

The word aprigraha means not gathering what one does not need. For everyday living certain necessities such as food, clothing and lodging are universal requirements. Nevertheless there is no requirement that they be expensive or exotic. The food that is eaten should be selected not only because it tastes good, but is also beneficial to one s health. Likewise, there is no need to overindulge in eating. Clothing should be comfortable and affordable and not worn for show, and it should not be hoarded.

If a person chooses to gratify all his desires, he will discover that there is no end to the list: a fancy and palatial house, a luxurious car, trips around the world, all kinds of entertainment. It just never stops. Chasing after the things one cannot afford or does not need merely produces an agitated mind and absence of peace and calm. Further, spending all of one s time satisfying one s personal pleasures and desires leaves little time to help others, pursue spiritual goals or practice yoga.

Aprigraha thus demands that we acquire less not more. Moderation in acquisition rather than catering to one s desires is the essential point. The race to acquire more and more not only never ends, it can never be satisfied. Breaking this vicious cycle and selecting a life of fewer needs and desires leads to mental peace and tranquility.

The five niyamas are as follows:

1. *SHOUCH:* Internal and external purity (previously discussed; see page 14).

2. *SANTOSH:* Contentment

Accepting whatever comes along in life with equanimity and contentment is the meaning of santosh. Contentment and peace of mind are essential in life and absolutely necessary to the pursuit of yoga. Being content and happy with what has earned through honest labor is santosh. This does not mean that one should avoid trying to do better or to get ahead, but it does mean that these goals should not be pursued if they bring unhappiness or discontent. Santosh is an extension of aprigraha. It suggests reducing ones needs and desires, becoming content with what one has and being helpful and generous to others. The inner joy that the person who is content with his lot in life experiences can never be acquired by someone who is always striving to acquire more and more material things. Such a person never has time to enjoy the things he has and cannot find time for peace, self-reflection and tranquility.

3. *TAPA:* Austerity

The word tapa is usually translated to mean austerity or asceticism and some have also implied the inclusion of harsh self-deprivation. For a period in his life, Buddha tried this kind of harsh self-denial by abstaining from adequate nutrition (it is said that he ate a single grain of rice per day) and found to his dismay that he merely became emaciated without any attendant enlightenment. In yoga, tapa implies the ability to withstand hunger when food is not available. This would also mean to be able to withstand heat or cold or other creature comforts without complaining. People who practice tapa learn to complete the tasks at hand. They do not give excuses or blame others for failure. Tapa implies the ability to endure any hardship in life's journey while pursuing God or the truth with joy and without complaint. Success in the pursuit of tapa requires mental, verbal and physical self-discipline. It means pursuing one's goals with patience, courage and integrity without faltering. Failure does not bring discouragement but the desire to try again. The practice of tapas provides focus in life and strengthens will power, both of which are needed for the successful pursuit of yoga.

4. *SWADHYAYA:* Study

The word swadhyaya means studying to acquire spiritual knowledge and the ability to think properly with an eye towards improving spiritual and mental well-being. Swadhyaya comprises two types: scriptural study and the study of self or introspection.

An aspirant to the practice of yoga is expected to study the Vedic Hindu scriptures such as the Vedas, the Upanishads and the Darshanas as well as other spiritual writings. Study does not include rote learning but demonstrating those lessons by incorporating them into the fabric of life. It is this incorporation that leads the aspirant along the sacred path to the attainment of God and to find bliss.

The second aspect of swadhyaya, self-reflection, means that each day the aspirant must evaluate the conduct of his life. Today did I lead a virtuous life and follow the spiritual path? Or did I drift toward vice or slip back? It is a lot easier to look at the shortcomings of others than to reflect on one's own. Until the aspirant is willing to take a daily honest look at his own behavior and make appropriate corrections, he will never make any real progress.

5. *EESHWAR PRANIDHAN:* Surrender to God (previously discussed; see pages 125–126).

STEP III: AASANA (ä'sunǝ pronounced aasun): Yoga postures, yoga exercises.

The word aasana in yoga terminology refers to those postures, or poses, of the body where the aspirant can comfortably and steadily remain without changing positions for some period of time while practicing yoga or meditating. A further requirement is that the body musculature be relaxed and devoid of tension so that there will be no discomfort or bodily distractions during the yoga practices. Whatever aasana is selected, it should never be forced or cause strain or discomfort, but rather be so natural that the yoga practitioner would be completely unaware of the posture he or she is in.

In both India and the West, the word aasana has frequently ended up being synonymous with yoga exercises despite the fact that Patanjali does not specify any postures or exercises. There are only three aphorisms concerned with aasanas (2: 46–48). The first of these states that the postulant should choose whatever aasana is most conformable and suitable, one in which he or she can remain for a length of time without either discomfort or distraction. The second aphorism says that perfection in any aasana is achieved by practice, avoiding strain and relaxing the body so that concentration on yoga is possible and achievable. The third aphorism affirms that with practice the ideal aasana will bring discipline of both body and mind. The person will be able to withstand physical discomforts, such as heat and cold, pangs of hunger so that the body's energy may be conserved for meditation and transformation into spiritual energy.

Various manuals describe many types of aasanas for the practice of yoga. Most often, the yoga teachers in India recommend *Sukhaasana*, the aasana of comfort. The aspirant sits cross-legged in a relaxed manner without attention to the position of the feet (either facing up or down) with the head, neck and spine in as straight a line as possible consistent with comfort. The hands either rest upon one another in the lap or over the respective knees with upturned half-opened grasp. The eyes are focused towards the midline just above the root of the nose, a place known anatomically as the glabella. Most beginners and many advanced yoga practitioners use this as the only aasana. The beginner usually starts by assuming this position for 10 to 15 minutes at a time and then gradually prolonging the period up to several hours. Variations on this aasana are the *Padamaasana* (lotus position) and one called the *Siddhaasana*. For those who have difficulty sitting cross-legged, the kneeling posture (*vajraasana*), or the posture of complete relaxation (*Poorn Vishramaasana*), which is executed by lying down, may be useful.

Complicated aasanas are not described in Patanjali's Yoga Darshana. These types of postures represent a later addition to the art of yoga and constitute a branch of yoga known as Hatha Yoga, yoga using force, or effort. Learning and practicing these postures is not essential to the core practice of yoga. These exercises are mainly used to assist the yoga aspirant in becoming healthier and stronger, as well as supple, thus allowing the practice of concentration and meditation to proceed for longer periods. As an example, *Shirshaasana* (standing on one's head) is regarded to be good for the brain as well as for strengthening the muscle of the neck and back. But it should be practiced for short periods, as it is not suitable for prolonged meditation. Further descriptions of other aasanas are in the reference by Swami Yogehwaranand Ji, which describes some 250 aasanas with photographs of many of them and explains their benefits. The other references, *Light on Yoga* by B. K. S. Iyengar, and *Yoga: Mind and Body* published by the Sivanand Society, also presents various types of aasanas, their variations and the benefits.

Hatha yoga is the main type of yoga taught in the West, especially on television and in yoga classes. These exercises should not be seen as an end in themselves but merely as a step along the road to the eight-step yoga.

The principal (root) text of Hatha yoga is Hatha Yoga Pradipika. (See reference section.) The text describes several complex aasanas and pranayamas (see below) as well as several difficult practices (*shat-kriyas* and *mudras*) to cleanse the body and accomplish perfection in yoga. While some of the practices of Hatha yoga seem to complement the core practices of Patanjali's eight-step yoga, many other are redundant, distinctly unnecessary, and some likely injurious to health (Hatha Yoga Pradipika 3: 85). Moreover, most teachings of Hatha yoga are akin to those of Puranas (see page 50) in contrast to the teachings of Patanjali's Yoga Darshana, which are based upon and are similar to those of the Vedas and Upanishads.

Of interest is the fact that the word *hatha* in Sanskrit not only means force or effort but also means being stubborn or obstinate. Some practitioners of Hatha yoga (especially in India) carry these postures to the extreme, doing such things as balancing the whole body on one hand or both, maintaining an unusual contortion or sitting on a bed of nails or thorns for long periods of time and calling themselves yogis (yoga masters). This is not real yoga but acrobatics performed for display and attention. True yoga requires virtuous conduct in life, meditation in quiet solitude and adherence to the principles of Yama and Niyama (or dharma).

STEP IV: PRANAYAMA: Control of the vital energy of the body and the breathing.

The word pranayama is usually translated to mean the controlled taking in and expelling of breath both for better physical well-being and for decreasing the agitation of the mind so basic to the practice of yoga. The word *prana* (pr'änə pronounced praan) as used in the Vedic scriptures and yoga means more than this. Prana refers to the subtle life force, the vital energy of the body. While every cell of the body is permeated by prana, it is not the same thing as soul. Every bodily function requires energy. In science, this is regarded as metabolic energy, an often-imperceptible form of energy that makes everything run. Breathing is only one of the indicators of the body's vital energy. According to pranayama it is the control and regulation of this subtle vital force that allows the energy to be conserved by reducing its expenditure. Prana is usually considered to have five separate forms:

1. *Prana:* Prana is the vital energy that controls the breathing. The cleaner the air we breathe, the more healthful it will be.

This is why experienced yogis recommend practicing yoga in quiet, peaceful places such as in the hills or near a stream or ocean, which are away from the noisy and more polluted environment of urban life.

2. *Vyana:* Vyana caries the vital life force (prana) to every cell in the body by means of the circulation of the blood. Vyana controls the functions of the heart and blood vessels.

3. *Apana:* Apana is that type of vital energy that allows the body to rid itself of waste products through the stool, the urine, and to a limited extent, through the sweat.

4. *Samana:* Samana is that component of vital energy that is needed for the digestion, absorption and metabolism of food.

5. *Udana:* Udana is that part of the vital energy that is required for the functioning of the nervous system, the brain, the spinal cord, the nerves and their connections (synapses).

Several breathing exercises have been described that strengthen each of the forms of prana. Three common and simple pranayama exercises are as follows:

1. *Rechak* (pronounced ray-chuck): Deep exhalation. This pranayama exercise is performed by slowly prolonging the exhaling of air until the lungs are empty.

2. *Poorak* (pronounced poo-ruck): Deep inhalation. This is performed by slowly drawing in the fresh air until the lungs are full.

3. *Stambhak* (pronounced stum-buck): Holding the breath. The breath may be held in three different ways: (a) holding the breath at the end of a complete exhalation; (b) holding the breath at the end of a deep inspiration; and (c) holding the breath at whatever place it may be at the time of the exercise.

Each of these pranayama-breathing exercises should be done with ease (preferably in an aasana) and never pushed to the point of discomfort. With gradated practice it becomes possible to prolong the duration of each breath during inhalation, holding the breath and exhalation. At first, prolonging the duration of each breath is a conscious activity, but with practice it becomes spontaneous and natural without discomfort or awareness of the process, even though the yoga practitioner may only be taking a few breaths per minute. As should be obvious, pranayama should be practiced in a calm and relaxed state and not during periods of excitement or following vigorous exercise when the brain and other vital organs of the body need extra breathing (oxygen) and holding the breath may be injurious to the health.

The practice of pranayama strengthens the physical body and makes it healthier as body systems work more effectively. According to Patanjali, steadiness in the practice of pranayama brings with it the ability to acquire knowledge and wisdom easily in any area one desires. The mind becomes calm and much less likely to wander with distractions, and concentration and meditation become easier. While performing pranayama, it is a good idea to meditate on God (Divine Spirit) or to silently chant God's name (OM). Both actions will help to steady the mind.

Books on Hath Yoga describe at least 50 other types of pranayama and their attendant benefits. Steady practice will allow the focus of the vital energy (prana) on any part of the body. The books also say that focusing the prana on the nervous system will awaken the *Kundalini* and gradually and progressively activate the eight chakkras so that one can advance in yoga and finally achieve samadhi. Kundalini is believed to be latent energy beginning at the lower end of spinal cord and ascending along the spinal cord to the brain. The eight *chakkras* are believed to be neurological centers beginning in the lower abdomen (in front of sacrum bone) and ascending into the brain. Detailed discussion of the activation of Kundalini and the techniques for progressing up the series of chakkras is beyond the scope of this book. There is some disagreement as to whether the chakkras described in Hatha Yoga represent valid neurological centers or plexuses (consisting of various nerves and neural ganglions including the sympathetic and parasympathetic neurological systems), or potential centers of vital energy only activated during the practice of advanced meditation (the latter is generally believed to be the correct interpretation). Patanjali does not mention either Kundalini or the chakkras in the Yoga Darshana, but commentaries on Hatha Yoga describe them in considerable detail. (See *Science of Soul* by Swami Yogeshwaranand Saraswati and *Hatha Yoga Pradipika*.)

Hatha Yoga texts place much emphasis on awakening of Kundalini and progressive activation by chakkras and consider them essential for progress in yoga. Many other yoga teachers who primarily follow Patanjali consider several Hatha Yoga's descriptions such as Kundalini or chakkras, imaginary and their pursuits as mere distractions of dubious merit.

STEP V: PRATYAHARA: Withdrawal from the stimulation of the senses.

The word pratyahara means the removal of the senses from their normal tendency to explore or be stimulated by everything that surrounds them that is either new or exciting. The yoga aspirant who has learned to control sensory attachments to things in the environment and to block attraction to vice is said to have victory over his senses. Once the mind is devoid of external stimulation, it can turn inwards and begin to concentrate and meditate.

For the person who has mastered pratyahara, it is possible to sit amidst a great deal of noise without being bothered or distracted by it because the stimuli of hearing have been withdrawn. It requires a very loud, prolonged or intense noise to cut through. This does not mean that the senses have become numb to stimuli and the person is unaware. Quite the contrary, even though the external input is shut down, the inner sensory and motor activities are highly activated. Thus, the perception of what is going on in the environment is still possible, should it be desired. If the individual wished to hear music this would be possible, as would the appreciation of subtle sensations of smell, taste, seeing and touch, as these abilities are highly activated.

Examples of this type of perception exist in the lives of Mozart and Beethoven. Mozart left no sketches of his music, but rather planned and heard the whole work mentally. Only when it was completed did he write it down. Beethoven is well known to have been deaf for much of his life but managed to compose symphonies, quartets and sonatas without apparent difficulty. These are examples of the activity of pratyahara.

STEP VI: DHARANA: Resolute mind, concentration.

Once the mind has withdrawn from the stimulation of the senses, it can focus on a single aim, goal or idea. This does not mean that it impossible to distract the mind from within, but rather that the mind has become committed to being focused and to concentrate. This commitment to concentration is the essence of dharana.

The main focus in yoga is to acquire spiritual knowledge. One can concentrate on the word OM with contemplation of its meaning or on a Veda mantra and understand its message. Alternatively, one can focus on finding the glory of God the Creator in various aspects of nature. It is also possible to use this focusing of the mind for the acquisition of secular or scientific knowledge as well. The focus can be also upon acquiring a talent and technique, such as in the case of an artist or musician.

During this stage, the practitioner begins by focusing on either a real or some imaginary object. Some yoga teachers instruct the aspirant to focus on a symbol of OM or a glow of a light in the mind or the glabella (part of the face between the eyes). Other teachers use an actual carving of symbol Om or some other religious object as the initial focus point. Initially, the concentration is on a large object, say a circle about the size of a basketball. This area of concentration is then gradually reduced until it becomes possible to stay focused for a long period of time on something as small as the head of a pin. The concentration gradually becomes so intense that, even with the eyes open, nothing is seen except the object that is being focused upon. This type of intense concentration is used by excellent athletes, such as archers, target shooters, golfers or basketball players. Archery students in India were taught to perfect their art by focusing their concentration only on the eye of the decoy (or bird) and the arrow and not on any of the surroundings, such as the landscape or even the body of the bird.

STEP VII: DHYANA: Meditation with intense concentration.

When the resolute mind can concentrate without interruption or distraction for a prolonged period of time it is in the state of dhyana. The practice of Zen Buddhism arose from the practice of dhyana in the Vedic Hindu religion. In the state of dhyana, so completely is the mind focused on a single goal that the contemplating person becomes unaware of his or her surroundings, even of the physical body.

A yoga aspirant in the state of dhyana has a singleness of purpose: to concentrate only on God and His attributes and the soul (the true self) separate from the body and mind (or ego). The important realization here is that God alone is Supreme Bliss and the only One who can enlighten our souls. Patanjali says that the practitioner must constantly repeat the word OM in his or her mind and meditate on its meaning because OM reflects God's attributes more completely than any other word. OM symbolizes that God is not only omniscient, omnipotent and omnipresent but also Sat-Chit-Anand, the Eternal Truth, the Supreme Consciousness and Supreme Bliss. (See pages 23–27.)

The meditation implies the following prayers: In You alone have we complete faith; we thank You, we honor You, we bow to You, we pay our respects to You and praise Your glory alone with all of our being. This kind of spiritual dhyana is true meditation. The mind is completely focused on God and experiences immense joy and serenity. In this state, medha budhi is highly activated and can acquire even more spiritual knowledge directly from God the Source of all knowledge (Yoga 1: 25).

During the state of dyhana, the mind is extremely sharp and can also be focused on the acquisition of secular knowledge. This type of intense concentration will allow the practitioner to easily learn any subject and will assist in the solving of difficult or seemingly impossible problems. A devoted scholar of secular knowledge during dhyana may make a new discovery or think of an invention, where as an accomplished musician during dyhana may compose a new symphony.

One must remember, however, that obtaining secular or spiritual knowledge does not ensure that a person will perceive God. God is perceived by the soul not intellect (Kathopanishad 2: 8). To be able to advance to the final step of yoga (samadhi) as a normal course of events, meditation is required as well as complete devotion and surrender to God.

During the practice of dyhana, it has been suggested that the if the mind is agitated or distracted by secular matters, it is not a good idea to force meditation. Instead, the individual should acquire a calm mind by withdrawing the senses from outside stimulation. Perhaps taking a quiet walk in a peaceful area would accomplish this. Another means of calming the mind might involve singing a devotional spiritual song. As stated earlier, repeated chanting of God's name while the mind is agitated or wandering everywhere is of little use. The mind must be calmed before true meditation may begin.

STEP VIII: SAMADHI: the superconscious state wherein God is revealed.

Samadhi is the final step in Raj Yoga. When contemplation of God (dyhana) becomes very intense for a long period of time, the individual loses sense of time and space, the physical body and emotions. He begins to see the true nature of the pure soul. God is beheld in His full glory as Supreme Radiance, Supreme Consciousness, the Source of All Knowledge and Supreme Bliss. This is samadhi. Samadhi is that superconscious state in which the individual soul comes face to face with the Supreme Soul and bliss as well as the end to all sorrows is achieved. The soul is said to be one with God. The soul attains God but does not merge with God or become God. The relationship of the soul and God in this stage of yoga is compared to that of an iron ball superheated in the fire to a red hot/golden yellow glow and the fire itself, respectively. The iron ball, looking like a fire ball, is one with the flame but is still and iron ball and not the fire itself. This is the state of perfection of the soul and the purpose for yoga.

Reaching samadhi once is not an end in itself. Patanjali states that samadhi must be re-entered for longer and longer periods of time to allow the yoga practitioner to advance and attain perfection. In this state, one's intellect is activated at the highest level called *prajna* (or *pragya*) and the soul easily obtains knowledge in any desired area directly from God. The enlightened soul will acquire extraordinary powers (see page 112) to be used only in the service of God and to help others and the world of nature. It must not be used for selfish reasons, sensual distractions or public demonstrations.

The soul must continue its concentrated effort to practice samadhi and dispassion in life—to finish the task of removing attachments and bondages. Through God's grace the enlightenment of the soul continues to progress until the only experience the yogi has is that of God. Everything at this point is God and His creation. The soul has continued to find liberation, peace and bliss and has finally attained God the Divine Consciousness.

APPENDIX

EVOLUTION OF PRAKRITI

Prakriti is described in many Veda mantras, the Upanishads and is presented in an organized manner in Sankhya, Nyaya and Vaisheshik Darshanas. (See pages 34 and 48–49 for details.) According to Sankhya Darshana, prakriti at its most primal level is composed of *mool tatwa*. The word mool tatwa means the most basic form of matter from which when activated by God evolve all components of the universe.[1] (Also see page 34 *Srishti*.)

Mool tatwa has three types of innate properties called *gunas*. These three *gunas* in the *mool tatwa* exist in a **balanced** state and their properties are as follows: *satwa* (full of energy but calm), *rajas* (full of energy but agitated) and *tamas* (inert, dull, no energy). Whether these three properties in modern scientific terminology may be translated to mean positive, negative or neutral respectively must remain conjectural for the present [see *Sankhya Sidhanta* (Sankhya Principles): a commentary on Sankhya Darshana by Acharya Uday Vir Shastri].

Following the activation of the primal matter (mool tatwa) arises an extremely minute subatomic form of matter called *mahat*. The word mahat means the primary or principal form of matter. This matter also forms the basis of our intellect. (See pages 117–125 for details on intellect/mind as used in Vedic scriptures.) From mahat arises the next level of matter called *ahankara*. The word *ahankara* means something with individual identity and forms the basis of our ego (see pages 123–124). In the creation of

---

[1]There are different opinions regarding what are the exact equivalents (both in the Hindi or English language) of the various matter forms that successively evolve from the mool tatwa.

matter, it would also imply the most basic matter that has individual identity. The matters called *mahat* and *ahankara* in Sankhya Darshan are considered to be subatomic. However, whether their size and form is at Bosons or Fermions (and their Superpartners) level or some other level is hard to decipher and at present must remain conjectural.

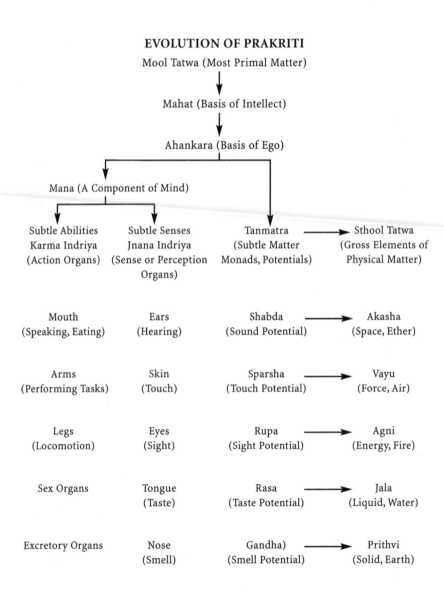

EVOLUTION OF PRAKRITI

Mool Tatwa (Most Primal Matter)

Mahat (Basis of Intellect)

Ahankara (Basis of Ego)

Mana (A Component of Mind)

Subtle Abilities Karma Indriya (Action Organs)	Subtle Senses Jnana Indriya (Sense or Perception Organs)	Tanmatra (Subtle Matter Monads, Potentials)	Sthool Tatwa (Gross Elements of Physical Matter)
Mouth (Speaking, Eating)	Ears (Hearing)	Shabda (Sound Potential) ⟶	Akasha (Space, Ether)
Arms (Performing Tasks)	Skin (Touch)	Sparsha (Touch Potential) ⟶	Vayu (Force, Air)
Legs (Locomotion)	Eyes (Sight)	Rupa (Sight Potential) ⟶	Agni (Energy, Fire)
Sex Organs	Tongue (Taste)	Rasa (Taste Potential) ⟶	Jala (Liquid, Water)
Excretory Organs	Nose (Smell)	Gandha) (Smell Potential) ⟶	Prithvi (Solid, Earth)

Following *ahankara* there are two offshoots of matter (see diagram). The first forms the basis of our perception in the form of *mana* or *manas* (see page 119) as well as our subtle inner senses and abilities (see page 13), which guide the functions of our sensory organs (*jnanaindriya*) and action organs (*karmaindriya*). (See pages 12–14.) From the second offshoot arise five *sookshma tatwas*, i.e., subtle physical matter called *tanmatras* (subtle matter, monads or potentials), and they may exist in the form of mass, force or space. *Tanmatras*, in turn, form the basis of next level of matter, which are the five *sthool tatwas* also called the five gross elements of nature/universe. (See below for details.) The five *sthool* (gross) tatwas are easily perceptible or visible to humans, however, the *sookshma* (subtle) tatwas, or *tanmatras*, are not. Manifest prakriti (*srishti*) exists as a combination of mahat and all its descendent, successive forms of matter (see diagram).

In contrast to Sankhya Darshan, in Vaisheshik and Nayaya Darshan the basic unit of prakriti (matter) is atomic called *anu* and each element made of anu has individual characteristics. These two Darshans do not describe mool tatwa.

The five *sthool* (gross) *tatwas* (elements) are Akasha, Vayu, Agni, Jala and Prithvi.

Akasha: The Sanskrit word akasha is usually translated to mean ether or sky. The word akasha at a subtle level, however, implies **space** and the sky is only one of the gross manifestations of space. Space is considered one of the most fundamental components of prakriti (matter), which pervades everywhere in the universe. It exists even at subatomic level between individual electrons as well as between electrons and protons or neutrons. The *tanmatra* (monad) for akasha is called shabda, and it is considered to be the medium of communication for word, knowledge or sound perception.

Vayu: The word vayu at a gross level means air or gaseous state. At a subtle level, however, vayu implies **force**, which leads to movement or flow from one point to another. Thus vayu would help any tatwa of prakriti to move or disperse away from one place to the other. Examples of vayu tatwa include air, windstorm, jet stream and the solar wind. The *tanmatra* (monad) for vayu is *sparsha*, and it is considered to be the medium of our sensory perceptions for touch, force or pressure.

Agni: The word agni at a gross level means fire or light. However, at a subtle level, agni implies the most basic component of all forms of **physical energies** in the universe. As such, this would include energy in the galaxies, stars (sun) or the earth; energy of fusion or fission; gravitational energy and heat or light energy. At the level of human body, it would include energy required for metabolism and other bodily activities. The *tanmatra* (monad) for agni is rupa, and it is considered to be the medium of sight or visual perception.

Jala: The word jala at a gross level means water or liquid phase. However, at a subtle level, jala implies the principle of **dissolving, mixing or interacting,** such as when chemicals react to form a new compound. Examples of jala are water, a solution in water, molten metal, liquid gas, an alloy, and a chemical reaction. The *tanmatra* (monad) for jala is rasa, and it is considered to be the medium of taste perception.

Prithvi: The word prithvi in Sanskrit at a gross level means earth or a solid mass. However, at a subtle level, prithvi implies the smallest particle of **matter that still has the special characteristics** of that matter and may exist in the form of an atom (anu), a molecule or a larger mass of them. Examples of prithvi are elements of the Periodic Table, any solid substance, earth. The *tanmatra* (monad) for prithvi is *gandha* and it is considered to be the medium of smell perception.

Our physical body is composed of mahat, ahankara, mana, subtle inner senses and action abilities (see above) as well as all five subtle (tanmatras) and gross tatwas. A log of wood has all five subtle and gross tatwas but no mahat, ahankara, mana, sensory or action abilities. A solid ball of iron at gross level is only prithvi tatwa, yet at a subtle level it has all the five subtle tatwas. For example, it has *akasha* in the form of space between the nucleus and electrons; *vayu*, (force) in the form of movement of electrons around the nucleus in electron clouds; *agni*, in the form of energy between protons and electrons, electromagnetic energy, gravitational energy, etc. It also has jala tatwa in iron's ability to melt as well as mix or react with other elements. Lastly, prithvi tatwa is present both at a gross and subtle level. The iron ball, being inanimate like the log of wood, has no mahat, ahankara, mana, senory or action abilities.

GLOSSARY

Aasana: Postures and exercises for yoga practice. Third step of eight-step yoga.

Ahankara: Identification of self; ego; vanity.

Ahimsa (also spelled Ahinsa): Non-violence, refraining from cruelty to others.

Akrodh: Controlling anger; one of the 10 virtues of dharma.

Anand: Bliss

Antahkaran: A generic word for mind, which includes all aspects of mind (also see ahankara, budhi, chit and mana).

Artha: Material or financial wealth.

Arya: A noble person who upholds virtue in all aspects of life.

Ashrama: Various stages in a person's life. The first 25 years for learning as a student; the next 25 years for being a house holder and raising a family; the next 25 years for contemplation and being a society elder; and finally spending the life beyond 75 years totally in the service of God and mankind.

Ashrama: Also means a holy place for retreat.

Asteya: Not to covet what belongs to others; one of the 10 virtues of dharma.

Asura: Unjust selfish persons.

Atma: Soul; also sometimes called jeev or jeevatma.

Bhakti: Devotion to God.

Brahma: God, another name for God the Creator of the universe.

Brahmacharya: Celibacy.

Brahman: God, another name for God implying He is the Greatest.

Brahmin: A spiritual teacher, one of the four major groups (varanas) of Hindu society.

Buddhi: Intellect at its most basic level.

Chit: Conscious, e.g., God, Soul.

Chit: The portion of mind primarily connected with emotions, desires and sanskars. At other times the word chit is also used for intellect or in a generic manner for all aspects of mind.

Darshanas: Darshans are philosophical treatises that reorganized in a systematic manner the messages of Vedas and Upanishads. There are six darshans namely Nyaya, Vaisheshik, Sankhya, Yoga, Poorva Mimamsa and Vedanta.

Deva: God; Saintly persons.

Dharma: Moral or virtuous way of living (in all aspects of life). Dharma (in Vedas or Hindu belief) is the closest word equivalent to the word religion in the West. Dharma is not an organized dogma or ritual. It encompasses 10 virtues namely dhriti, kshama, dama, indriya nigraha, shouch, asteya, akrodh, vidya, dhee and satyam.

Dharana: Yoga step where one practices concentration of mind so that mind becomes resolute and focussed. Sixth step of eight-step yoga.

Dhee: Intellect with ability to discriminate between right and wrong; wisdom; one of the 10 virtues of dharma.

Dhira: A wise person.

Dhriti: Thoughtfulness with patience and strength; one of the 10 virtues of dharma.

Dhyana: Yoga step where one meditates with intense concentration. Seventh step of eight-step yoga.

Dama: Disciplining or self-control over mind; to become a master of mind and not its slave; one of the 10 virtues of dharma.

Eesha (also spelled Isha): God, Master of all spiritual and material wealth of the universe, Universal Benefactor.

Eeshwar: God, Universal Benefactor.

Eeshwar pranidhan: Surrender to God, a major requirement for advancement in yoga.

Guru: A master teacher who furthers the spiritual and secular knowledge of the pupil.

Hatha Yoga: Yoga using force; branch of yoga devoted to physical and breathing exercises; the type of yoga usually taught in the West.

Indriya: Indriya means sense organs (ears, eyes, nose, tongue and skin) and action organs (arms and hands, legs and feet, mouth to eat and talk, sex organs and excretion organs).

Isha: See Eesha.

Ishwara: See Eeshwar.

Jnana (also spelled Gyana): Knowledge (especially spiritual).

Kama: Desires (as a generic term), sometimes translated as sexual desires.

Karma: Deeds, actions.

Krishna: Great Hindu king, master yogi and warrior during Mahabharata era who by many (perhaps most) Hindus is regarded and worshiped as an incarnation of God.

Kshama: Forgiveness; one of the 10 virtues of dharma.

Kshatriya: A warrior, one of the four major groups of Hindu society.

Mahabharata: *Mahabharata* is one of the two major epics of India that record the great war of ancient India called Bharata in those days.

Mana (also spelled Manas or Manah): Mind. The word mana sometimes is used as a generic word that includes all aspects of the mind. Whereas at other times, it is exclusively used for that component of antahkaran which brings messages to soul via sense organs and carries out the will power of soul via action organs.

Mantra: Hymns of Vedas and sometimes also of related scriptures. Mantra is not a secret incantation or a secret formula.

Manu: Manu is believed to be the

first law giver of India and his commentaries are recorded as Manu-smriti.

Manushya: Average human being.

Moksha: Attainment of God and ultimate spiritual bliss as well as where cycle of reincarnation is broken for a very prolonged time.

Nishkama karma: Karmas or deeds done in a selfless manner with no desire for anything in return. Such karmas do not bind a person; instead they liberate because they are done in the service of God.

Niyama: Moral observances, disciplines of life. Second step of eight-step yoga.

Om: God. God in Vedic Hindu scriptures is called by many names depending upon the particular attribute that is given. However, the word Om is strictly reserved for God alone. Om is considered symbolic of God being Universal Benefactor and Protector as well as Omnipresent, Omniscient and Omnipotent.

Paramatma: Supreme Soul, God.

Patanjali Rishi: Holy seer who is the author of Raj Yoga aphorisms, i.e., the eight-step yoga.

Prakriti: Physical matter.

Pranayama: Control of breathing and vital energy of body. Fourth step of eight-step yoga.

Prarthana: Prayer to God.

Pratyahara: Yoga step where mind is withdrawn from external stimulation by senses so that it can concentrate inwards toward realization of soul and reaching God. The fifth step of eight-step yoga.

Puranas: Hindu scriptures that describe the legends, myths and folklore of ancient India.

Raj-yoga: The traditional eight-step yoga of India according to Patanjali rishi.

Rama: Hindu king and hero of epic Ramayana who by many, perhaps most, Hindus is regarded and worshiped as incarnation of God. Hindus consider his human form and manner to be the ideal person that one should try to emulate; he is also thought to be the ideal husband and ruler.

Ramayana: *Ramayana* is the epic story describing Rama's life and his rule.

Rishi: Holy seers, sages, advanced yogis who have accomplished samadhi. The Vedas were first revealed to rishis.

Samadhi: The highest step of yoga meditation where mind is in a superconscious state and where a person finds self-realization and attains God and bliss. Samadhi is not a trance-like state as is usually described in English-language dictionaries in the West.

Sanskar (also spelled Samskaras): Root impressions of karma (in the mind) that remain with the soul until attainment of moksha or liberation.

Santosh: Contentment.

Sat: Eternal; truth, good.

Satsang: Hindu congregation; literally means the company of truth seekers and truth followers.

Satya or Satyam: Truth. One of the 10 virtues of dharma and a component of the first-step (yama) of eight-step yoga.

Shouch: Purity of mind and outer cleanliness. One of the 10 virtues of dharma.

Shradha: Faith in and devotion to God based upon truth (in contrast to blind faith).

Shruti: Shruti are Vedic Hindu scriptures that are believed to have been revealed by God and include the Vedas, Upanishads and related scriptures.

Shudra: Laboring class; one of the four major groups of Hindu society.

Smriti: Smriti are Vedic Hindu scriptures recorded by man.

Stuti: Praise and love of God, singing glory of God.

Swadhyaya: Study of scriptures and introspection (study of self).

Tapa: Practice of austerity so that one can withstand material deprivations.

Tatwa: Elements of prakriti, i.e., physical universe.

Upasana: Meditation, communion with God.

Upanishads: Philosophical commentaries based upon the teachings of the Vedas.

Vairagya: Dispassion and renunciation, a major requirement for advancement in yoga.

Vaishya: Farmers, business people, traders, artisans; one of the four major groups of Hindu society.

Vedas: The root source of all Hindu scriptures; collection of about 20,000 hymns that are believed to have been revealed by God to rishis (seers) in the state of samadhi. They discuss spiritual as well as secular subjects. They are organized into four branches Rig (knowledge), Saam (devotion), Yajur (action) and Atharva (science).

Vedic: Based on the Vedas; that which pertains to the Vedas.

Vidya: Knowledge including both spiritual and secular (the latter in Vedas and Upnishads is sometimes called avidya). One of the 10 virtues of dharma.

Viveka: Discriminative knowledge that enlightens a person to see things as they really are and to follow truth and virtue in life.

Vritti: Mind's activities and inclinations that cause its agitation. They must be calmed so that the mind can become tranquill and one can progress in yoga.

Yama: Self-controls, abstention from vices. First step of eight-step yoga.

Yoga: Meditation that enables the soul to attain God and find ultimate bliss. It is of four types Raj Yoga, Bhakti Yoga, Karma Yoga and Jnana (Gyana) Yoga.

Yog Sutra: Yoga aphorisms, recorded by Patanjali rishi.

SELECT REFERENCES[1]

SECTION I: BASIC BELIEFS OF HINDU RELIGION

A: General References published in Hindi and/or Sanskrit only

1. Swami Dayanand Saraswati: *Satyartha Prakash*. Jhajjar, Haryana, India: Haryana Sahitya Sansthan 1983. (This book was first published in 1882, since then several publishers have published it).

2. Swami Vidyanand Saraswati: *Satyartha Bhaskar* Part I and II. Bombay: International Arya Foundation 1992.

3. Krishan Kumar: *Cultural History of Ancient India*. New Delhi: Shri Saraswati Sadan Publications 1993.

A: General References in English.

1. Durga Prasad: *Light of Truth* (an English translation of *Satyartha Prakash*). New Delhi: Jan Gyan Prakashan 1972. (This book was first publihed in 1908).

2. Swami Prabhvanand: *The Spiritual Heritage of India*. Hollywood, California: Vedanta Press of Southern California 1963.

3. Anthony Basham: *The Wonder that was India*. New York: Grove Press Inc. 1959.

4. G. Feuerstein, S. Kak and D. Frawley: *In Search of the Cradle of Civilization*. Wheaton Illinois: Quest Books 1995.

B: Definition of Dharma: Hindi and Sanskrit only

1. Sushila Anand: *Dharma Tatwa*. New Delhi: Self-Published 1993.

---

[1]Please note, this is a select list of references that the author found most useful in writing this book. Also, the order of the references is based on usefulness rather than the traditional alphabetic order. The author used several other references in writing this book, but their inclusion was considered unnecessary.

C: What is Eternal in Hindu Religion: Hindi and Sanskrit only

1. Acharya Uday Vir Shastri: *Sankhya Sidhanta*. Delhi, India: Vijaykumar Govindram Hasanand 1991.

2. Viveka Bhushan Darshanacharya: *Tatwa Gyan*. Sabarkantha, Gujrat, India: Darshan Yoga Mahavidyalaya 2000.

D: Vedas and Related Scriptures: Vedas in Hindi and/or Sanskrit only

1. Swami Jagdishwaranand Saraswati: *The Vedas*. Delhi, India: Vijaykumar Govindram Hasanand 1997. (This book includes all 20,349 Vedic Mantras organized in the four separate Vedas. The book also has an alphabetic index for all of them. There is no Hindi or English translation of any mantras.)

2. Swami Dayanand Saraswati: *Yajur Veda Bhasha Bhashya*. New Delhi: Sarvadeshik Arya Pratinidhi Sabha 1975. (This book was completed in 1882 and first published in 1889. Since then several publishers have published it.)

3. Pandit Harisharan Sidhantalankar: *Saam Veda*. New Delhi: Arya Samaj Ramakrishnapuram 1973.

4. Pandit Harisharan Sidhantalankar: *Atharva Veda Bhashyam* Part I and II. Delhi, India: Bhagwati Prakashan 1990. (Part I & II include Sanskrit Hindi Translation of about half of Atharva Veda. Part III & IV to be published in future.)

Vedas in English and Sanskrit

1. Swami Satya Prakash Saraswati and Satyakam Vidyalankar: Rig-Veda Volume I to XIII. New Delhi: Veda Pratishthana 1977 to 1987.

2. Swami Satya Prakash Saraswati and Satyakam Vidyalankar: *Saam-Veda* Volume I and II. New Delhi: Veda Pratishthana 1991.

3. Swami Satya Prakash Saraswati and Uday Vir Viraj: *Yajur Veda* Volume I to III. New Delhi: Veda Pratishthana 1994.

4. Swami Satya Prakash Saraswati and Uday Vir Viraj: *Atharva-Veda* Volume I to V. New Delhi: Veda Pratishthana 1996.

5. F. Max Muller: *Rig-Veda Sanhita*. London: Trubner & Company 1869.

Upanishads: in Hindi and Sanskrit only

1. Pandit Bhimsenasharmana: *Upanishada-samuchhaya*. Jhajjar, Haryana, India: Haryana Sahitya Sansthan 1981. (The book contains all of the principal Upanishads; it was first published in 1933.)

2. Mahatma Narayan Swami: *Kathopanishad*. New Delhi: Sarvadeshik Arya Pratinidhi Sabha 1980. (The book was first published in 1934.)

3. Mahatma Narayan Swami: *Mandookyopanishad*. New Delhi: Sarvadeshik Arya Pratinidhi Sabha 1981.

Upanishads: in English and Sanskrit

1. Sarvapalli Radhakrishnan: *The Principal Upanishads*. London: Unwin Hyman Limited 1953.

2. Swami Satyam: Kathopanishad: *Be Loved by God and Conquer Death*. San Diego: California, Vedic University of America 1993.

3. Swami Satyam: *Mandookyopanishad*. San Diego California: Vedic University of America 1994.

E: Smriti (Hindu) Scriptures: Manu Smriti: in Hindi and Sanskrit

1 Pandit Harishchandra Vidyalankar: *Manu Smriti*. Delhi, India: Vedic Dharma-Shastra Prakashan Sanstha 1959.

Itihasa (History): in Hindi and Sanskrit

1. Swami Jagdishwaranand Saraswati: *Mahabharatam* Part I, II and III. Delhi, India: Govindram Hasanand 1991.
2. Swami Jagadiswaranand Saraswati: *Valmiki Ramayana*. Delhi, India: Vijaykumar Govindram Hasanand 1995.

Itihasa (History): in English

1. Kamala Subramaniam: *Mahabharata*. Bombay: Bhartita Vidya Bhavan 1980.
2. Kamala Subramaniam: *Ramayana*. Bombay: Bhartiya Vidya Bhavan 1981.
3. J. E. Schwartzberg and S.G. Bajpai: *A Historical Atlas of South Asia*. Chicago: University of Chicago Press 1978.

Gita (Bhagvad Gita): Hindi and Sanskrit

1. Swami Vidyanand Videh: *Gita-Yog*. Ajmer, India: Veda Sansthan 1978.
2. Swami Sampurnanand Saraswati: *Shrimad Bhagvad Gita*. Merrut, Uttar Pradesh, India: Radhey Lal Sarraf & Sons Charitable Trust 1983.

Gita (Bhagvad Gita): English and Sanskrit

1. S. Radhakrishnan: *The Bhagvadgita*. London: George Allen & Unwin Ltd 1949.

Darshans: in Hindi and Sanskrit

1. Acharya Uday Vir Shastri: *Sankhya Sidhanta*. Delhi, India: Vijaykumar Govindram Hasanand 1991.
2. Acharya Uday Vir Shastri: *Sankhya Darshan*. Delhi, India: Vijaykumar Govindram Hasanand 1995.

3. Swami Jagadishwaranand Saraswati: *Shad-darshanam* (all six Darhanas together). Delhi, India: Vijaykumar Govindram Hasanand 1994.

F: *Other Hindu Religious Texts*

1. G. N. Das: *Select Kabir Dohas*. Bombay: Bhartiya Vidya Bhavan 1992.

SECTION II: 40th CHAPTER OF YAJUR VEDA

Hindi or Sanskrit

1. Pandit Harisharan Sidhantalankar: *Ishopanishad*. Delhi, India: Pusa Satsang 1961.

2. Swami Dayanand Saraswati: *Yajur Veda Bhasha Bhashya* 40th Chapter. New Delhi: Sarvadeshik Arya Pratinidhi Sabha (publisher) 1975. (This book was completed in 1882 and first published in 1889. Since then several publishers have published it.)

3. Mahatma Narayan Swami: *Ishopanishad*. New Delhi: Sarvadeshik Arya Pratinidhi Sabha 1988.

English-Sanskrit

1. Swami Satyam: *Win the battle of Life* (40th Chapter of Yajur Veda). San Diego, California: Vedic University of America 1989.

2. Swami Vidyanand Saraswati: *Ishopanishad*. Panipat, Haryana, India: Vedic Shodha Samsthan 1992.

3. Swami Gambhiranand: *Eight Upanishads* Volume I. Calcutta: Advaita Ashram 1989.

SECTION III: YOGA

Hindi-Sanskrit

1. Acharya Uday Vir Shastri: *Patanjal-Yoga Darshan*. Delhi India: Vijaykumar Govindram Hasanand 1994.

2. Acharya Uday Vir Shastri: *Abode of the Soul in the Physical Body in Vir Tarangini* (by same author). Delhi, India: Govindram Hasanand 1992.

3. Mahatma Narayan Swami: *Yoga Rahasya*. Delhi, India: Sarvadeshik Arya Pratinidhi Sabha 1993.

4. Swami Atmanand Saraswati: *Sandhya Ashtanga Yoga*. Jhajjar, Haryana, India: Haryana Sahitya Sansthan 1982. (This book was first published in 1934. This book also discusses the abode of the soul in the physical body.)

5. Swami Satyapati Parivrajak: *Yoga Mimamsa*. Sabarkantha, Gujrat, India: Darshan Yoga Mahavidyalaya 1999.

6. Gyaneshwararya: *Yoga-Darshanam*. Sabarkantha, Gujrat, India: Darshan Yoga Mahavidyalaya 2000.

7. Swami Vidyanand Saraswati: *Abode of the Soul in the Physical Body in Deepti* (by same author). Delhi India: Vijaykumar Govindram Hasanand 1995.

8. Swami Yogeshwaranand Saraswati: *Bahiranga Yoga*. Rishikesh, Uttar Pradesh, India: Yoga Niketan Trust 1970. (This book was first published in 1961.)

9. Swami Yogeshwaranand Saraswati: *Atma Vijnana*. Rishikesh, Uttar Pradesh, India: Yoga Niketan Trust 1972. (This book was first published in 1959.)

10. Swami Yogeshwaranand Saraswati: *Brahma Vijnana*. Rishikesh Uttar Pradesh, India: Yoga Niketan Trust 1964.

English-Sanskrit

1. Tulsi Ram: *Patanjal Yogadarshan*. Jhajjar, Haryana, India: Haryana Sahitya Sansthan 1989.

2. Pandit Nardeva Vedalankar: *What is Yoga?* New Delhi: Jan Gyan Prakashan 1973.

3. Swami Satyapati Parivrajak: *Simplified Yoga for God Realization*. New Delhi: Aryasamaj Vasant Vihar 1997.

4. Swami Hariharananda Aranya: *Yoga Philosophy of Patanjali*. Albany, New York: State University of New York 1983.

5. B. K. S. Iyengar: *Light on the Yoga Sutras of Patanjali*. New Delhi: Harper Collins Publishers India Pvt Ltd 1993.

6. Swami Prabhvanand and Christoper Isherwood: *How to Know God: The Yoga Aphorisms of Patanjali*. Hollywood, California: Vedanta Society of Southern California.1953.

7. Swami Yogeshwaranand Saraswati: *First Steps to Higher Yoga*. Rishikesh, Uttar Pradesh, India: Yoga Niketan Trust 1970.

8. Swami Yogeshwaranand Saraswati: *Science of Soul*. Rishikesh, Uttar Pradesh, India: Yoga Niketan Trust 1972.

9. Swami Yogeshwaranand Saraswati: *Science of Divinity*. Rishikesh, Uttar Pradesh, India: Yoga Niketan Trust 1974.

10. B. K. S. Iyengar: *Light on Yoga*. London: George Allen & Unwin Ltd 1966.

11. Ian Whitelaw and Irene Lyford: *Yoga Mind & Body*. London: Sivanand Yoga Vedanta Centre 1996.

12. Pancham Sinh: *The Hatha Yoga Pradipika*. New Delhi: Munshiram Manoharlal Publishers 1997 (This book was first published in 1915).

DICTIONARY

1. Suryakanta: *Sanskrit-Hindi-English Dictionary*. New Delhi: Orient Longman Limited 1975.

INDEX

Order Form

The Essence of the Hindu Religion

☐ Yes, I would like to order ——————— books at $12.50 ea.
+ shipping + applicable sales tax.
Volume discounts are available for multiple copies. Please inquire.

I understand that I may return any books for a full refund
(except shipping), for any reason within 30 days.

Mail orders: ASK Publications
P.O. Box 29182
Los Angeles, CA 90029-0182
Telephone: 323-664-8078
E-mail: askpublications@yahoo.com

Name: _____

Address: _____

City: _____ State: _____ Zip: _____

Telephone: (_____) _____

Sales Tax: Please add 8.25% for books shipped to California addresses.

Shipping: $4.00 for the first book and $1.00 for each additional book. All
books shipped via US priority mail.

Payment: ☐   *Check or Money Orders Only*

Order Form

The Essence of the Hindu Religion

☐ Yes, I would like to order ——————— books at $12.50 ea.
+ shipping + applicable sales tax.
Volume discounts are available for multiple copies. Please inquire.

I understand that I may return any books for a full refund
(except shipping), for any reason within 30 days.

Mail orders: ASK Publications
P.O. Box 29182
Los Angeles, CA 90029-0182
Telephone: 323-664-8078
E-mail: askpublications@yahoo.com

Name: ————————————————————————————

Address: ———————————————————————————

City: ————————————— State: ————— Zip: —————

Telephone: (———) ————————————————

Sales Tax: Please add 8.25% for books shipped to California addresses.

Shipping: $4.00 for the first book and $1.00 for each additional book. All
books shipped via US priority mail.

Payment: ☐ *Check or Money Orders Only*